D1446856

Changing Dimensions in International Education

Changing Dimensions in International Education

F. Robert Paulsen, Editor

The University of Arizona Press
Tucson Arizona

THE UNIVERSITY OF ARIZONA PRESS

Manufactured in the U.S.A.

S. B. N. 8165-0190-4
L. C. No. 73-76783

Contents

Foreword

In an era when concern over any field of emphasis no longer can be considered as exclusive to any one territory, education finds itself operating on ever-broadening horizons. In this volume, therefore, each presentation focuses either on a significant aspect of the changing dimensions of international education, or on the trends in the developments of education within the nations selected.

The authors represent vast experience in the fields of international and comparative education. Most of the contributors hold professorships in Comparative Education within their respective institutions. As a result of its increasing interest in international education, the federal government has called on these authorities, among others, to be the leaders in the development and maintenance of programs stimulating a better understanding of education as an international concern.

The presentations in this volume originally were created for the 1966-67 Colloquium Series of the College of Education at the University of Arizona. Appreciation is given to each author for the lecture itself as well as for the submitted manuscript.

I acknowledge appreciatively the assistance of Mrs. J. Raymond Gerberich, who read all manuscripts and offered valuable suggestions in the final editing, and the work of Mrs. Beryl J. Barney, who typed both the initial and final drafts. We also express appreciation to the University of Arizona Press for its competence in final staging and production in book form.

F. ROBERT PAULSEN

About the Authors

Dr. Victor H. Kelley, Senior Professor in the College of Education, University of Arizona, is known and respected by the thousands of students with whom he has had contact during thirty years of teaching. During his career, Dr. Kelley has held assignments in almost every phase of the curricula in teacher-education. He has been active in many professional associations, including the Association for Supervision and Curriculum Development and the American Educational Research Association. For years he served as sponsor of the University chapter of Phi Delta Kappa, national honorary education fraternity.

During the past decade, Dr. Kelley has become a world traveler, studying the educational systems of various nations in Africa, Asia, and Europe. In writing about "Education Upon the Seven Seas," Dr. Kelley describes a fascinating experience as well as a new concept of the dimensions of international education. The theme of the voyage was "Joining Humanity's Quest," which assumes that man in all ages and all cultures has sought something that relates to education or is attainable through it.

Dr. Gordon I. Swanson, Professor of Education at the University of Minnesota, has become well known as an American educator interested in international affairs. Dr. Swanson has served as a consultant of the World Bank Mission to Afghanistan, the Ford Foundation Vocational Education Mission to Brazil, and to the Educational Policies Commission of the National Education Association. He is a member of Phi Delta Kappa's Commission on Education, Manpower, and Economic Growth, and has served as president of Phi Delta Kappa International.

Dr. Swanson believes that education has never been studied in a perspective appropriate to the cultural development of nations of the world and that recent national legislation enables American educators to contribute to the educational development of any country needing assistance.

Dr. I. N. Thut, Professor of Education at the University of Connecticut, is acclaimed for his scholarly and authoritative contributions in the areas of Comparative Education and the History of Education. A frequent visitor to Europe, Professor Thut has written about many of the educational developments on the Continent. In "Higher Education in Western Europe in the Twentieth Century," he observes that the institutions of higher education in Europe, with centuries of historical tradition, are becoming more and more like the universities found in the United States.

Dean Neville V. Scarfe, born and educated in England, is one of Canada's most distinguished educators. He has served as Dean of the Faculty of Education at the University of British Columbia since 1956, and is a member of various associations, boards, and commissions concerned with the development of education in the Canadian Provinces. In addition to his achievements in the field of teacher-education, Dean Scarfe also is a well-known geographer.

In "Education in the Canadian Provinces," Dean Scarfe predicts an improved form of progressive education in the next few years.

Dr. Herbert B. Wilson, Professor of Education at the University of Arizona, serves as an advisor to the International Student Club and as faculty-sponsor to the Fullbright International Teacher Development Program. He has conducted several educational study tours in Mexico and, since 1964, has been director of the Arizona-Sonora Student-Teacher Exchange Program. The latter program involves students in the College of Education at the University of Arizona and those attending the Normal School in Hermosillo, Sonora. Dr. Wilson spent the year 1955-56 at the UNESCO Fundamental Education Center at Patzcuaro, Mexico, on a grant from the U.S. Department of State. His enthusiasm for developing educational programs across the Southwest and in Mexico is well known.

In his survey of "Education South of the Border," it is apparent that Professor Wilson is convinced of Mexico's potential leadership among all Latin American countries in both education and general cultural development.

Dr. Hugh B. Wood, Professor of Education at the University of Oregon, is probably the best-known American in the land of Nepal. He served as director of a University of Oregon-Agency for International Development Contract Program in Nepal during 1954-59, and has returned to the Himalayas many times. Many Nepalese educators continue their educations at the University of Oregon under the guidance of Professor Wood. Their studies emphasize ways by which they might develop the educational programs in their own country.

"Education in the Land of the Yeti" indicates the monumental task confronting the people who live in the Himalaya Mountains today.

Dr. Marsden B. Stokes is Professor of Education and Director of the Bureau of Educational Research and Service at the University of Arizona. Dr. Stokes has been a teacher, principal, superintendent of schools, and Deputy State Superintendent of Public Instruction for the State of Utah. During 1962-65, Dr. Stokes served as Chief-of-Party of the University of Utah-Agency for International Development Contract at the Haile Selassie I University in Addis Ababa, Ethiopia.

The continent of Africa is in a period of educational, economic, and political ferment. In "The New Education in Africa," Dr. Stokes describes the confrontation between the old patterns of instruction, which over-emphasized content while giving little attention to the learner and his needs, and the new education, which promotes a philosophy of humaneness not acceptable to many of the parents in the nation.

Dr. Stewart E. Fraser, Professor of Education and Director of the International Education Center at George Peabody College for Teachers, is a native of Australia and holds degrees from institutions in his native country as well as in England and the United States. He is a member of Phi Delta Kappa's Commission on International Relations in Education, the Comparative Education Review Editorial Board, and the Educational Committee of the United Nations Association of the U.S.A.

One of the most interesting political paradoxes in the mid-twentieth century has been the confrontation between Communist China and the Soviet Union. This political confrontation has affected the educational relationships of the two countries. It is well known that education in Communist China is in a state of flux, but it is not well known or understood that political influence has directly affected educational programming there. Some of the information discussed by Dr. Fraser in "Sino-Soviet Educational Relations" cannot be documented in the usual way as it has been drawn from radio dispatches and fragmented information available through a censored press.

Dr. Anoop Chandra Chandola, Assistant Professor of Oriental Studies at the University of Arizona, was born and educated in India. He pursued advanced studies at the University of California at Berkeley, and the University of Chicago. Dr. Chandola is a member of the Association for Asian Studies, the Linguistic Society of America, and the Linguistic Society of India. He has presented papers at many international conferences in the area of his specialization and has authored many publications, most of which have appeared in scholarly journals in the United States.

Dr. Chandola discusses several of the serious problems confronting India today, the most significant of which are its education and economic standards. In "The Challenge to Higher Education in India," Dr. Chandola indicates that while education can transform a nation, India will change only if a certain national lethargy is eliminated and the citizenry accepts the responsibility of living a productive life.

Dr. A. M. Gustafson is Director of Pupil Personnel Services in Tucson School District No. 1, in Tucson, Arizona. He has served as an elementary and junior high school teacher, and as a principal. Dr. Gustafson holds membership in many educational organizations, including Phi Delta Kappa, Comparative Education Society, American Association of School Administrators, and the Arizona Pioneers' Historical Society.

In 1959, under the sponsorship of the American Association of School Administrators, Dr. Gustafson visited the Soviet Union for the first time. Subsequent visits included educational tours sponsored by the Comparative Education Society and the International Commission of Phi Delta Kappa. From these visits, Dr. Gustafson gained an interest in Soviet education, as well as considerable information about what is fact and what is only rumor about the Soviet Union.

International Education: Portents for the Future

Gordon I. Swanson

There are many facets of the broad subject known as international education. As many educators are interested in comparing national systems of education and each has his own opinion of what international education should be, international education is not easy to define. In simple terms, we might use a functional definition: international education is the specialty of the comparative educator. The comparative educator is engaged in the accumulation of knowledge about educational systems around the world. And, although this is a complex task, international education is not an area exclusive to the specialist. The study of international education is of interest to every educator who desires a broader perspective of educational philosophy and, indeed, the educational enterprise in general. It is an important area of human inquiry and can lead us to a deeper understanding of the common humanity of man.

In recent years, international education has become an interesting and fruitful field for study. One of the reasons for its growth has been the rapid advances in communication technology. Modern means of communication have effectively reduced the size of our world and widened our horizons of concern. The shrinking of our globe makes cultural isolationism impossible. Today, man is moving toward a world civilization; because of this, he needs to conceive a universal system of education. But what should the principal features of such a system be? That is a difficult question, and it is one on which few educators can agree. Needless to say, a universal system of education should have a common curriculum. But what should be the content of the curriculum? This is another "sticky" question. The answers to these questions are far from clear; nevertheless, there is a principle that might prove to be useful in our search for some answers – a universal system of education will have to be based on the common elements in human experience. A universal system of education will have to select from the "pool" of human experience that knowledge deemed to be of greatest value. Such an education will have to enhance the common humanity of man.

In a search for the common interests of mankind, education must be conceived as having a broad base and unlimited horizons. Education must be more than transmission of knowledge. There must be concern with the crucial problems of our time. Education must give us a common point of view. In this sense, then, international education must be concerned with the improvement of humanity. Education, like the Archimedean lever, can be used to move the world. Education is the instrument by which man shapes his social being, the process by which he molds his mind. Education expands the range of man's consciousness. It provides him with the conceptual system through which he views the world. And in the present age, this conceptual system must further international understanding. For if it does not, man may not be around to view much of anything.

Modern societies have become dependent on education. This reliance on education is reflected in the large number of people who are engaged in the educational enterprise. In the United States, for example, more than three million people are involved in our institutions of learning. This figure is more than the combined employment totals for the industries of steel, aerospace, and electronics. And in some of the world's underdeveloped countries, the relative size of the educational undertaking is even greater. In Nigeria, for instance, educational institutions employ some 125,000 people. This figure represents a sizable part of that country's total population, about equal to the number of people engaged in Nigerian industry. Thus, in the modern world, education has come of age. It is clearly the proper business of man.

The magnitude of modern education is closely related to the growth of the nation-state. Indeed, education has become one of the primary concerns of every modern state; because it has, the ends and means of education have come to reflect national aspirations. Education, in short, has been molded by the spirit of nationalism. Hence, it has not always served the end of international understanding. But in an attempt to escape from the ethnocentrism of merely national concerns, the United States Congress in 1966 passed the *International Education Act*. This act marked a significant step in the direction of international understanding. If this legislative program succeeds, our institutions of higher learning will acquire a new dimension. Universities will become increasingly international in outlook. And at last, those working in higher education will accept the ideal of Comenius, the great Moravian educator, who pointed out the pansophic character of learning. As Comenius saw it, higher education should be concerned with all knowledge. Higher education should be free from national bias, and it should be truly universal.

It is time to consider central propositions. The following propositions provide the structure for the presentation:

(1) International education must promote scholarship and learning.
(2) International education has to facilitate economic and social development.
(3) International education can and must lead us to a better understanding of man.

Education Must Promote Scholarship and Learning

Scholarship and learning are the basic conditions of all knowledge. The desire to know is the universal basis for education. There cannot be education without both knowledge and the means to learn. These factors are also the cornerstones for international understanding. The ideal of scholarship has always been transcultural. It has never been a purely national phenomenon. Thus, if we are to make progress toward world understanding, educators must rise above mere national concerns. Educators must promote scholarship and learning on a truly international scale. Hence, programs in international education such as conferences, exchanges, and fellowships all make a positive contribution toward international understanding.

In addition to this, if education is to be the means by which standards of international amity are promoted, there must be avoidance of the traditional cultural dichotomy between East and West. Our schools can no longer treat world history as if Western culture had a monopoly on events of the past. (And, we must admit that world history has been taught as if it began with Egypt and culminated in a "pax-Americana" around the world.) This faulty view of the richness of the human experience must be replaced by a broader concept of history. The study of world history must develop an understanding of peoples who live in Africa and Asia as well as peoples in the Western hemisphere. Modern education must formulate a curriculum that is more representative of man's total experience. The curriculum cannot be hemmed in by traditional ties. Education must furnish a universal concept of man.

In addition to this broader view of history, education must make the fruits of scholarship and learning universal. Essentially, all knowledge is the collective product of the human mind and it is the proper inheritance of all mankind. If international education can make knowledge universal, it will bring about a renaissance in our time. The importance of this renaissance is apparent – if it should come to pass, scholarship will be able to expand its horizons to a world view and mankind will be on the threshold of a new intellectual era. In this era, science and technology could provide the means by which man could shape this planet in accordance with his fondest dreams. The expensive burden of war would be eliminated from the international scene and the world would become, at last, a friendly home.

International Education Has To Facilitate Economic and Social Development

The promotion of cultural change is one of the implicit goals of international education. International education seeks to modify existing cultural patterns. One of the ways to modify a given culture is through the process of diffusion. The diffusion of cultural traits is as old as mankind. Man has always been interested in borrowing useful cultural traits from other groups of people. At the present time, however, cultural diffusion has come to mean helping less developed countries acquire technological skills, and developed nations have begun to compete for spheres of influence in the underdeveloped world. Since World War II, this competition for spheres of influence has gone on at a feverish pace. The United States and Soviet Union have each spent billions of dollars (or rubles) each year in diffusing the blessings of their respective systems. This "proselytizing" tendency on the part of modern nations is a subtle form of cultural paternalism. If technological development is to contribute to international understanding, education must be used to better replace such political motives with more enlightened reasons for change.

Modern history has witnessed a quickening pace in social and economic change. And yet, our conceptual systems for understanding this change are sorely inadequate. We need new and better theories about our world. Consider, for example, the fundamental causes for economic development. At one time, it was believed that economic development was tied to institutional patterns. Thus, by changing institutional forms, one could facilitiate economic growth. This theory leaves much to be desired. A more recent theory has related economic development to the availability of an abundant supply of natural resources and it has been argued that no country could be developed unless it possessed a vast supply of raw material wealth. Needless to say, there are numerous examples that contradict this theory. What is the reason for economic growth? We really do not know. We are certain that the whole process is very complex but we do not have a comprehensive theory to account for all of the factors involved.

Although the process of social and economic development remains a mystery, the role of education in furthering this process is clear – no country has developed very far without a highly educated and trained population. The training of manpower is an economic investment which produces economic returns just as surely as does an investment of capital. The development of human resources, then, is intimately related to the economic growth of nations. It is the medium through which all significant changes must be transmitted. And if this is so, then the development of human resources is the surest way to further social and economic change. There can be no development apart from the development of man. Indeed, man may be the measure of all things.

In recent years the world has witnessed a new social phenomenon that has altered the balance between available resources and necessary space. This phenomenon is overpopulation. At one time, the world was both underdeveloped and underpopulated. This is no longer true. Much of the world is now faced with the problem of being overpopulated as well as underdeveloped. And what is more crucial, it is the underdeveloped world where the population explosion is most serious. The problem of overpopulation raises many grave questions for education. The birth rate in underdeveloped countries tends to cancel out any gains made toward a developed society. Man has put a "chain" around his neck – the "chain" of his own reproduction.

In addition to the problem of overpopulation, the modern world has witnessed another new social phenomenon – the proliferation of nation-states. Since World War II, Africa and Asia have promulgated a whole series of new countries. In all of these countries the rate of illiteracy is very high and there is a crucial shortage of trained manpower. Most of these new countries do not have people trained to develop the natural resources at their disposal. Massive education programs are needed, but education costs money and underdeveloped countries do not have the economic base to support the extensive programs required. Clearly, the only sure answer seems to be in the form of financial and technical aid from the more developed nations of the world.

The less developed countries of the world seem to have placed their trust in education as an instrument of social and economic development. For, as the less developed countries look at the developed world, they see the reliance placed on education. Leaders of these underdeveloped nations jump to the conclusion that more and better education is the answer to all of their problems. This conclusion is shortsighted, since most of the advanced countries did not deliberately plan their educational systems with the goal of social and economic growth in mind. Rather, their educational systems just grew like "Topsy." In many ways, education afforded pragmatic answers to historical problems. The question, therefore, is whether education is the cause or the effect of cultural development; at the present time the answer to this question is far from clear.

International Education Can and Must Lead Us To A Better Understanding of Man

We now come to a final consideration. It is proposed that the study of international education can lead us to a better understanding of man. An insight into the nature of man is one of the fringe benefits gained from the study of international education. Indeed, cross-cultural analysis is one of the best ways of seeing man in all of his cultural complexity. The knowledge of another educational system provides us with a mirror in which we can better view our own image. International education furnishes us with information about alternative possibilities; through this study we gain an understanding of our own educational provincialism and glimpse the common humanity of man.

The current interest in international education is not of temporary concern. It is not a passing phase in the educational spectrum. The study of international education has deep roots and represents one of the basic desires in man's intellectual being – the desire for common cultural goals. In the pursuit of these goals, our schools have a central role. Thus, it is little wonder that we are demanding more from our schools. We have placed them at the very center of our hopes for the future; if they do not come up to our expectations, we shall be in for a rude awakening.

A final point is that there is a need to create educational institutions that cut across national boundaries. The intellectual community needs an "educational marketplace" for the development and testing of ideas. We can no longer continue in the smug ways of the past. National systems of education are inadequate for the challenges of our time and must create new institutions to bridge the gaps created by a strict nationalism. Education must be viewed with international perspective. Education must become truly universal if we are to realize the common humanity of man.

Education Upon the Seven Seas

Victor H. Kelley

The nature of such a subject as "Education Upon the Seven Seas" suggests the need for some explanation. I spent the spring semester of 1966 serving as a faculty member on "The Floating Campus," the *MS Seven Seas*. This educational project is under the Seven Seas Division of Chapman College, Orange, California, in cooperation with the University of the Seven Seas Foundation. During this semester, we sailed around the world, leaving Los Angeles on February 10, 1966, and docking in New York City on June 17. We visited seventeen ports on this voyage. The assigned title might be paraphrased "Endeavoring to Understand People in Other Countries While Earning College Credits." This is a unique venture – education combined with travel.

In America, we have thought that we are independent and isolated from the rest of the world. We have so persistently thought of ourselves as being self-sufficient that many times we have failed to realize that we are, and always have been, living in an interrelated world. When the first immigrants came to this country in the early part of the seventeenth century, they brought with them concepts of education that had been developed in their native countries. This was evident in 1636 when Harvard was established in Massachusetts. Certainly Harvard was modeled after those colleges existing in Cambridge and Oxford. As early as 1647, a law was passed in Massachusetts making it necessary for towns to establish a school system modeled upon the English pattern. The

Dame School, the Latin Grammar School, and the Writing Schools were carryovers from a European heritage. The trend in the ensuing years, however, was away from an educational system patterned after those found in Europe: communication with the old country was difficult, and distinctly American institutions began to develop – for example, the academy, the public high school, and our own type of liberal arts college.

In the mid-nineteenth century, the United States again looked to Europe for leadership in educational development. In his famous "Seventh Report," Horace Mann extolled the virtues of the European (particularly the Prussian) educational system. This emphasis aroused controversy with the Boston school masters, and thus his report was probably more widely discussed than it otherwise might have been.

By 1870, our own internal difficulties – culminating in the Civil War – had curtailed extensive contacts with Europe. But toward the late 1800's, we were again looking to Europe for educational ideas. Birdsey Northrop wrote an article, "Should American Youth be Educated Abroad?", in which he stated that "the present year (1873) has witnessed an unprecedented exodus of our youth to Europe."[1] He further commented, "The fancied superiority of European schools, the supposed economy of living on the Continent, and a vague ambition for foreign culture, have alike contributed to this result. More than all, fashion has given its sanction and created a furor in favor of European education. Example is contagious. The multitudes now departing are likely to draw thousands more."[2]

Northrop then criticized European education, and one notes that a number of American school officials reviewed and reacted to his proposition that a foreign education was detrimental to an American youth. In general, his reviewers (including such people as Eliott of Harvard, Hopkins of Williams, and Angell of Michigan) agreed with him, and suggested that only after a young person had gained considerable maturity would it be advisable for him to go to Europe to study.

---

[1]Birdsey Northrop, *The Evils of a Foreign Education*, ed. Stewart Fraser, International Center, George Peabody College for Teachers (Nashville, Tennessee, 1966), p. 1.
[2]*Ibid.*

The vast number of immigrants who came to this country from the late 1870's until 1914 certainly afforded students in the United States considerable familiarity with the products of European education. There is little in the literature to indicate that there was any great displeasure during these years about the youth of our country receiving an education in Europe. The United States entered World War I in 1917, and by the end of that year, many of our young men were going to Europe "to make the world safe for democracy." For the first time, great numbers of our youth had an association with people in a foreign country. Many a young man returned to the United States with a resolve to revisit Europe as soon as possible. In the early 1920's the "cattle boat" technique was used for visiting Europe, and there was a considerable exodus of students to study on the Continent. In the late 1920's, there was at least one floating university trip around the world. The trip was apparently a success, but the stock market crash and depression prevented any significant expansion of the plan at that time. World War II virtually stopped all travel to Europe.

The entry of the United States into the war in 1941 again necessitated our sending tens of thousands of young men (and this time, many of our young women) to Europe. Although many of our military men returned from Europe in 1945, we began placing our troops on a defense perimeter around the world. At the same time, we embarked upon a plan for exchanging students – a plan which far exceeded anything dreamed of before.

Programs for the exchange of students were developed by many agencies, including the Institute of International Education, the American Institute for Foreign Study, and the Junior Year Abroad. Philanthropic foundations, such as Rockefeller and Ford, joined the surge to communicate across cultures. Other plans included work and study projects by the government, churches, and educational institutions, such as the Peace Corps, Crossroads Africa, Teachers for East Africa, Youth Work Camps, National Education Association Travel, and Comparative Education Field Seminars. Many universities and colleges sponsored "travel with study" as part of their regular offering. Certainly, the experience of traveling has now become as reputable as it is acceptable in earning university credits.

Cynthia Parsons, Education Editor of the *Christian Science Monitor*, commented:

Should students in United States colleges spend one of their four undergraduate years studying in another country? When students who have studied abroad are asked this question, they usually respond affirmatively, and then qualify their answers by adding, "Of course, it all depends on the student." Professors and college administrators are not at all sure that students should spend an academic year abroad, especially if it is considered one of the four leading to a bachelor's degree. The majority feel that, while the year is good for learning a second language, it does not contribute to the basic academic growth of most students.[3]

At this time, however, we might consider a specific and unique program involving study and travel.

Chapman College of Orange, California, has an organized program known as "The Seven Seas Division." It receives support from the administration, the faculty, and the students, as well as from independent financial resources. While sponsored by Chapman College, this division recruits its student body and faculty each semester from many different colleges and universities across the country. The students are registered as are any other Chapman College students, and the courses taken are on the college records.

The project was actually conceived by a group of Rotarians from Whittier, California, who formed a nonprofit corporation, the Seven Seas Foundation. The maiden voyage was made in 1963, and was evidently a huge success as it was immediately followed by others.[4] The Department of Education of the State of California authorized transcripts for those who completed the work, but it was difficult to gain acceptance of these college credits. The answer seemed to be in asking an established college with proper accreditation to assume the administration of the program. In 1965, Chapman College accepted this responsibility, and is now responsible for the administration per se.

The general purpose of the trip I am reporting was to view educational and social problems in the various countries visited, and to relate the observations, experiences, and discussions of the students to general academic considerations.

---

[3]Cynthia Parsons, *Christian Science Monitor*, Feb. 4, 1967, p. 9.

[4]Donald D. Davis, "Around the World with the Floating University," *Rotarian Magazine* (June 1964).

The complete trip was accomplished in 126 days, with almost half of the time being spent in port cities. When one considers an educational experience involving 325 students from 90 different colleges, with faculty members recruited from different sections of the country, and classes being held on sailing days in whatever area of the ship seemed most suitable or available, the undertaking seems somewhat fantastic.

The following countries were visited in order: Tahiti, New Zealand, Australia, Singapore, India, Ceylon, Kenya, French Somaliland, Egypt, Lebanon, Syria, Israel, Greece, Italy, Algeria, Morocco, and the Maderia Islands. Field trips inland were always arranged so that a broader view might be obtained than one confined to the port city itself. The trip was made on the Holland-American ship known as the *Seven Seas*, a 13,000-ton vessel. Space on the ship was leased to The Seven Seas Division of Chapman College, Orange, California. The theme for the semester was "On a Quest of Humanity." A regular schedule of classes was organized with courses in such areas as English and Foreign Languages, Drama, Art, Speech, History, Economics, Political Science, Sociology, Philosophy, Education, Mathematics, Marine Biology, Oceanography, and Astronomy. Classes were in session each day except Sunday as the ship sailed from port to port. Slightly more than half of the total number of days was actually spent in class work.

The final examination and review evaluations were conducted between Madeira and New York City. Several fundamental questions were raised by those of us who served as faculty and staff members as we contemplated this program:

1. Can there be satisfactory academic work accomplished under such conditions as limited library facilities, crowded quarters, and completely new faculty and students?
2. Is it possible to teach subjects so that activities in each port will enhance and enrich the students' study?
3. Is it possible to orient and direct more than 300 students, some still in their teens, to insure the best possible experience without some of them becoming involved in the seamy and sordid part of port cities?
4. Will students moving quickly in and out of a port city gain anything beyond a superficial awareness of the city?
5. Will the American college student be able to make contacts in a port city that will enable him to pursue any special interest of his own?

6. What types of decorum and conduct can one expect from students on board ship, as well as on shore?
7. Finally, would students find any greater challenge for themselves in life than they would if they had remained on the college campus?

It is very difficult to answer adequately the first question concerning the academic quality of the program. While library facilities may have been limited, most came to the conclusion that students on board ship were much like those registering for classes at stateside universities. Some of the students failed to find anything in the library that had any bearing on a topic of study; others were very discerning, and if they did not find the precise material needed, they were able to substitute and interpret the things they did find. Students were heard to say: "I did not find any direct reference in the library, but I did find such and such. I am going to remember this and when I return to my own campus, I will look further."

In some areas, the academic work was definitely enhanced by the port activities. I am certain that the course in Comparative Education benefited tremendously by going ashore and communicating with people from education offices, by visiting schools in port, and by talking to students in the port about their educational backgrounds. Obviously, the course in Marine Biology was easily taught – the ship occasionally stopped in mid-ocean to permit class members to bring up samples for study.

Living in close quarters (an unavoidable part of living on board a ship) made it easy to engage in conversation. Sometimes this was a handicap, and the academic pursuit may have suffered at the expense of "just talking." However, at times students discussed their assignments with each other in a way that might not have been possible upon a land-based campus, and this seemed advantageous. Many professors had the experience of students meeting them following a lecture or discussion and saying, "I did not understand fully what you said today in class." Thus, additional time was spent in clarifying viewpoints and lectures, much more than the time usually available in our stateside colleges and universities schedules.

We have noted that the program was organized so that there would be positive experiences gained in port activities. In effect, these activities were of three general types:

First, the activities were organized in advance by the College authorities and all students and faculty participated. The trips were planned carefully, and usually were sufficiently extensive to need bus transportation. For example, a trip into the rural area of New Zealand afforded an opportunity to see something of the economy of a rural area in that country, and to observe certain techniques of farming, ranching, and the production of agricultural commodities.

Second, individual instructors organized specific activities relating to an individual class. For example, the Comparative Education class visited and conferred with the Ministry of Education in several countries, and the students visited several schools in session.

Third, some resourceful students made contacts on their own. One economics major interested in banking presented himself at various banks and gained a great deal of information through his own efforts. Similarly, faculty members were able to enrich their own experiences.

In addition, all students aboard were required to take a course called Sociology-Area Studies. In some respects, participation in this course was the highlight of the entire academic program. Experts in the history and geography of each country lectured to the students prior to arrival at each port. Faculty members always attended these lectures, and discussions followed.

Visiting lecturers and professors were brought aboard at nearly every port. Regular faculty members having a special interest and information about the various ports were called upon to present material on their specializations.

Finally, visitors were brought aboard at each port, and personnel of the U.S. Embassy or Consulate met with the students and faculty in almost every country.

One great concern of the administration and faculty related to the students' leisure time on shore. This was particularly true where the mores and customs of the people differed tremendously from our own standards and customs. Fortunately, there were people on board who had already been in almost every port visited on this voyage. They briefed the entire student group, and attempts were made to help the younger students realize that the information did not come as lectures from their elders, but from their peers who had previously observed the difficulties and problems in terms of their own inexperience. Every effort was made to help the students realize that the image of the United States would be reflected by their behavior. We are proud to report that our students responded nobly.

Many university contacts were made by students; several times they were entertained at receptions and dances given by their peers in the port cities. Some chaperonage was furnished by the administration, but there was a distinct effort made to let students chaperone themselves.

One example of a young person's involvement and understanding was found in the experiences of a young Papago Indian—a senior from an Arizona collegiate institution. Some friends had seen the possibility of creating a favorable atmosphere if a "first American" could take along little gifts to give selected representatives of countries visited. Joe made a great impression by giving trinkets and products of the Papago people to the Tahitians, the Maoris, and others, as the ship stopped at various countries. In turn, because of these presentations, he received invitations to visit and confer with governmental representatives. In a sense, he was envied because of the opportunities afforded him for discussions with people of other races, and it is certain that Joe came away with a much clearer understanding of those countries we visited than many of the more sophisticated but limited travelers of the group.

Another experience that amazed faculty and administration was the invitations received by individual students to visit in private homes. These visits were most valuable and certainly surpassed the ordinary type of exposure afforded the summer traveler to a foreign country.

A few days in a port obviously cannot permit even the most sophisticated to gain any great understanding of the problems of a city or a country. It was of concern to many faculty members, therefore, that students might obtain only a superficial understanding of the various peoples visited. While there were evidences of an inadequate awareness of many critical problems, there were also many examples of discernment among students, and indications that lasting insights had been obtained.

For example, while the students no doubt enjoyed the Tahitian dancers, most of them were more interested in reporting such facts as the effects on the economic life of the Tahitians or the nuclear explosion proposed by the French. And they observed that France had a surplus of personnel whose disproportionate food consumption produced a devastating effect on the economy of those islanders who did not work for the French. Further, students who had an interest in various socioeconomic problems seemed to make contact in almost every city with leading officials who could give them information about the problems. (One could never cease to marvel at the ingenuity of the students in ferreting out sources of information in the countries visited.)

Living in close quarters aboard ship might create problems, and it did, but the number of incidents of unbecoming conduct on shipboard were relatively few. The combination of faculty and student responsibility was very effective. Students elected their own officers who were expected to assume the same type of responsibilities usual on any land-based campus.

The students themselves enforced much of the discipline needed. The ship itself was a "dry" ship, alcoholic beverages not being permitted. The "bar" was a place where soft drinks, candy, cigarettes, and coffee were dispensed. Relatively few infractions of the nonalcoholic rule were discovered throughout the semester. No particular effort was made to police the activities of students ashore, but returning to the ship under the influence of alcohol was a severe offense and was disciplined accordingly.

The theme of the voyage in the Sociology-Area Studies class was "Joining Humanity's Quest." This theme assumed that man in all ages and in all cultures has sought or quested something or some things. It was hoped that the students would test this assumption as they moved from culture to culture and from nation to nation. I believe that many students did evaluate themselves in the light of their own culture as well as in terms of man's total history and culture. Many students testified in conversations, in class discussions, and in papers that they did develop a sense of belonging to a world community and a world culture. More important, they realized that they were a part of it.

Dr. Desmond W. Bittinger, Dean of the floating campus, "The Seven Seas," in discussing this attitude, said:

> Their questioning emerged gradually as they learned to identify more and more fully with fellow students in a score of the nations of the world. In this

student relationship all inhibiting lines such as color, nationality, language, religious belief, or even age group tended to disappear. The mutual awareness of being students over-rode all such usual barriers. Moreover, the American student, somewhat to his surprise, meshed into this world student group at a position lower than the top. He discovered that he entered it somewhat crippled in comparison to others. He knew only one language, one money system, and, in comparison with the others, very little world history and geography; his greatest handicap, however, was that he started with the assumption that it was not important that he know these things. He awakened to the fact that really he had been in the world but not of it! By and large, this is the sad condition of the American adult as well. Some widely traveled Americans, including American politicians, insist on remaining within this crippled group.[5]

As the faculty and students prepared to embark at the last port of call, Funchal, Madeira, many students were heard to say, "Oh, I wish that I could stay on here forever." But as they neared New York City, they became excited about arriving home. The students, like the faculty, had experienced a wonderful time but were eagerly awaiting a glimpse of the lady guarding the harbor at New York. A comment often heard was, "I'll never be the same again."

Indeed, we had been on a successful quest for humanity!

[5] Desmond W. Bittinger, *Messenger*, Church of the Brethren, Oct. 13, 1966, p. 9.

Higher Education in Western Europe in the Twentieth Century

I. N. Thut

It may appear anomalous for a paper on European universities to begin by calling attention to the uncertainties and perplexities that presently are plaguing higher education in the United States. The fact is, however, that we are interested in European university education precisely because there is widespread concern over the present status of our own colleges and universities. Perhaps there is also a haunting fear that in the midst of sweeping societal change, we should review standards of "academic respectability" which by habit we have imported from abroad.

Two previous periods in our national development produced comparable changes in American higher education. In the first period, the colonial colleges were ushered in. They have remained with us as the highly prestigious "Ivy League Schools." As is well known, they were not exact copies of the then existing European universities. Rather, they were small, fractional parts of certain of those universities, parts that were particularly attractive to the American Protestant community.

The second period of radical change in American higher education occurred approximately one hundred years ago. This period gave us public colleges dedicated to strengthening our secular philosophy of education. This form of higher education was also inspired by European example, in this case the newer

German universities. Indeed, it is estimated that as many as ten thousand Americans traveled abroad in the nineteenth century to acquire what was then known as the elements of the new learning. Many returned with European Ph.D. degrees. Those who had earned them at German universities became active in transforming certain colonial colleges and most of the state schools into universities by adding graduate studies and instituting the practice of awarding earned graduate degrees.[1]

In view of the formative influence exerted by European universities it is not surprising that as today's much heralded "tidal wave" of young people seeking admission to our colleges and universities is spilling over the entrance gates, and our intellectual foundations are being shaken by an appalling list of political, economic, and social crises, we are turning eastward once again to see if the old, familiar sources of institutional example and scholarly counsel might yield yet another morsel of wisdom suited to our present moment of need.

Origins of the University Tradition

University education in the United States is scarcely one hundred years old. In contrast, the oldest European universities will soon celebrate their eight-hundredth anniversary as degree-granting institutions. This difference in age alone would account for much of the influence European scholarship and intellectual traditions have exerted on the American institutions.

In his monumental work on the medieval university, Rashdall stated that, "The universities and the immediate products of their activity may be said to constitute the greatest achievement of the Middle Ages in the intellectual sphere. Their organization and their traditions, their studies and their exercises affected the progress and intellectual development of Europe more powerfully, or (perhaps it should be said) more exclusively, than any schools in all likelihood will ever do again."[2]

History indicates that as the power of the Holy Roman Empire and the Roman Church diminished in Western Europe, the

[1]Everett Walters, "The Rise of Graduate Education," *Graduate Education Today* (Washington: American Council on Education, 1965), p. 6.

[2]Hastings Rashdall, *The Universities of Europe in the Middle Ages* (Oxford: The Clarendon Press, 1936), I, 3.

universities continued to stand near the seat of authority. Protestant sovereigns became particularly aggressive in extending their protection to the universities within their domain, and in establishing new ones; some of their Catholic brethren did almost as well.

Although considerable information is available concerning the development of universities during the Renaissance, the Prussian reforms of the nineteenth century have specific relevance to those institutions continuing into the current era. Following the Napoleonic Wars, Prussia moved to gain firm control of education in order to use it as one of its most important tools for the restoration of political control.[3]

A national ministry of religion, education, and public health was created as a major branch of the royal government. Teachers were made civil servants. Their training, certification, and appointment were assigned to a new agency called the *Schulkollegium* which was created for this purpose and operated at the provincial level. Distinctive and separate roles were assigned to the vernacular reading schools, the grammar schools, and the universities with a view to reducing the wasteful duplication of effort that had prevailed. Universities were stripped of their *Paedogogiums* and the subuniversity activities and the instruction formerly offered therein were assigned to the secondary schools.

An even more drastic change was made in the university structure by abolishing the faculties of arts. This was done by designating that part of the arts curriculum which preceded the first (or bachelor's) examination as preparatory studies, and assigning it to the secondary schools. The second part, which formerly had led to the master's examination, was broken into fragments and each of the four remaining faculties took over whatever places it thought useful as an introduction to its program of professional studies.

It was this action, inspired by political considerations, and for reasons of economic efficiency, that led to the dismemberment of the faculties of arts in the Continental universities and, consequently, to the disappearance of the bachelor of arts and master of

---

[3]For a vivid account of these developments see Frederich Paulsen, *Geschichte des gelehrten Unterrichts* (Berlin: Walter de Gruyter, 1921), II, 286-301.

arts degrees. Needless to say, the private liberal arts colleges in America, notably the Ivy League schools which were already in existence at that time, did not choose to follow Prussia's rather drastic example; from this circumstance many of the present differences between European and American higher education can still be traced.

The Prussian government, however, was interested in still other reforms that promised to improve the efficiency of their schools as they were being mobilized to serve the goals of the state. The royal ministry had become suspicious that far too many parents were enrolling their sons of military age in the schools and universities merely to avoid conscription. Eliminating the arts faculties from the universities had closed one popular haven for the suspected draft dodgers, but the numerous municipal, ecclesiastical, and other secondary schools were still open to them. Indeed, many of these schools now became even more attractive as they added the first part of the arts curriculum that the universities were forced to relinquish. To deal with this loophole, the government prepared a short list of the most reputable and exclusive secondary schools and placed them under royal protection, support, and control. Thereafter, these elite schools, and only these few, were permitted to be called *Gymnasien*. A single-track curriculum was prescribed for them that consisted of the classical Latin and Greek languages and literature, and the philosophical elements of rational humanism including inductive logic in the form of elementary mathematics. All other schools were forbidden to teach Latin; hence, no other schools could prepare students for admission to the universities. Nor could their students claim exemption from conscription for military service. Perhaps we should note once again that these so-called educational reforms were largely motivated by the ambitions of the military planners in Prussia as the *Junker* class joined with the Hohenzollern nobility in their historic drive for world power.

There is time to mention only one other measure adopted by the Prussians to make education a more efficient tool of the royal government. We refer to the introduction of a system of external examinations by means of which the monarchy was able to control the flow of students from the newly reorganized *Gymnasien* to the stripped-down universities. Known as the maturity examination, or *Reifeprüfung*, and administered by the *Schulkollegium,* the royal government could now manipulate the examinations so as to determine not only how many would be permitted to enter the universities each year, but also to whom this coveted privilege would be extended.

To understand better the purpose of the maturity examinations and the manner in which they were used, it must be remembered that prior to the Prussian reorganization, each university, or more correctly, each faculty of a given university, formulated and administered its own admission policies. Historians have noted that the faculties were adept at interpreting their policies with whatever leniency was required to keep their lecture halls filled. Students of American higher education will recall that the colleges in the United States have enjoyed much the same privileges from their beginning. But after 1807, the Prussian rulers were not disposed to permit this easy way of life to continue and by instituting the maturity examination system, they stripped the universities of their historic control over admission procedures.

Universities in the Twentieth Century

By 1900, the academic community in Europe had been profoundly affected by the Prussian models of education. Prussian military and diplomatic achievements during the nineteenth century indicated an almost unbroken series of triumphs over her neighbors. The role of education in making these achievements possible was speedily recognized. Thus, educational reorganization in imitation of the Prussian model soon occurred in nearly all parts of Western Europe. That is to say, by the beginning of the twentieth century, universities on the Continent had lost their faculties of arts and were restricted to the four professional faculties, namely, law, medicine, philosophy, and theology. In a few places, as in France where a separation of church and state occurred, even the faculties of theology were excluded from the universities. Those that continued to exist did so as private establishments under ecclesiastical support and control. Administratively, the reformed universities thus became agencies of the state and the instructional staffs were employed as civil servants. From this time on, no university or faculty of a university could add a chair or appoint a new staff member on its own authority.

That is to say, European universities in the twentieth century are state institutions and for the most part are administered as political branches of their central governments.

University admissions are now administered externally by means of state-sponsored examinations. These examinations have become known by various names such as the *abitur*, the *baccalaureat*, and the General Education Certificate Examination, as well as the *Reifeprüfung*. From their beginning in Prussia, these examinations have been based on the classical languages and literature, and inductive philosophy. These are the subjects that the rational humanists of the nineteenth century considered to be the only ones that afforded the intellectual discipline necessary to assure success in university studies. The examinations are expected to ascertain whether the applicant has reached the necessary intellectual maturity or, as the Germans call it, *die Reife*, the concept that has characterized these examinations as "maturity examinations" even to this day.

In view of the subjects covered in the maturity examinations, admission to them soon was limited to students who had spent the necessary years in an approved preparatory school. Known by such names as *Gymnasium, Lycée, Colegio, Collège*, or Grammar School, depending on the country in which they were located, these preparatory schools were placed under close state supervision if not outright control. By 1900, all teachers for these schools were prepared in a university faculty of philosophy. In France, designated members of the faculty of philosophy of the regional university were made responsible for preparing and reading these examinations; thus they controlled admission to university studies in all the faculties. In German states, the examinations were prepared and administered jointly by representative teachers in the *Gymnasien* and representatives of the provincial educational authority known as the *Schulkollegium*.

Although the official preparatory schools generally received relatively generous public support, it was their practice to charge rather high tuition fees. These fees, and other social barriers, served quite effectively in restricting admission to the sons of the right families. And since these schools afforded the only path to university studies, their classical curriculum and the maturity examinations, together with the professional faculties of the universities, came to constitute a three-stage system of neatly articulated educational institutions by which the artistocratic governments in power at the beginning of the twentieth century could assure themselves a supply of just the right number of politically safe administrators to staff the governmental bureaucracies, clergymen to fill the pulpits of the state churches, military officers and surgeons to run the armed forces, and teachers to staff the system of select secondary schools and the universities. That is to say, schools and universities were made to contribute in a very direct and important way to the perpetuation of the established class system and the efficient operation of the aristocratic governments in power. By the time of World War I, European universities functioned largely as bulwarks of tradition rather than as specialized agencies affording intellectual leadership in the search for new knowledge by which men might improve their social institutions and themselves.

In all fairness, however, it must be noted that even as this familiar institutional pattern was hardening into tradition there were rumblings of discontent within the academic community. Even as Prussia was developing into a military state, the need for a strong economic base to support the military establishment was recognized and a premium was placed upon the scientific knowledge that would make such a base possible. The revolutionary curriculum pioneered by the University of Berlin in 1810 was a direct result of this interest; in a very short time the faculties of philosophy at other universities (chiefly, in neighboring German states) had also added chairs in geology, physics, botany, and other so-called pure sciencies.

But the major burden for scientific studies and technological applications was placed on new types of institutions regarded as somewhat inferior to the universities. These are the technicums and polytechnical institutes, the *École Grandes* of France, and the *Fachschulen* and *Technische Hochschulen* of the German states. From the outset, their graduates were awarded diplomas as distinguished from degrees, for they were not thought capable of providing intellectual leadership in the search for knowledge, at least not in the manner approved by the rational humanists who continued to dominate the faculties of philosophy. Such students of science and technology were looked upon as technical specialists, persons who could make things run without necessarily knowing why or to what purpose. That is to say, the hereditary elite were not about to share social control with the rising commercial and industrial classes by granting the graduates of the scientific schools status equal to the graduates of the universities.

Two additional changes affecting university education throughout Europe occurred in the German Empire (the successor to Prussia) prior to World War I. The first change occurred when separate schools for girls were opened, under private auspices, which duplicated the curriculum of the *Gymnasien* for boys. In due time, pressures were created to admit girls from these new schools to the maturity examinations. A few were admitted experimentally and unofficially, with results that proved highly disturbing to the traditional concept of masculine supremacy in academic matters. In time, several of these schools for girls were accredited as preparatory schools and their graduates were admitted to the maturity examinations on the completion of a course of classical studies identical in content, but one year longer than the regular course prescribed for the boys.

Having breached this wall, an occasional woman was then allowed to enter certain university lecture halls, literally by a side door, and by World War I, a few universities were admitting women openly – not merely as auditors, but as matriculated students and occasionally even as candidates for degrees. Since then, European universities have generally been coeducational institutions. Coeducational preparatory schools were rare, however, and have continued to be so even to the present time.

The second change of note came as lectures in the pure sciences were added by the university faculties of philosophy. This addition was tolerated by the university communities even though it was recognized that the scientific studies employed a philosophical method of inquiry radically different from that of the rational humanists who dominated the faculties of philosophy. In universities where this methodological difference created serious problems, as at the University of Bern in Switzerland, the faculty of philosophy was divided into two separate groups, one of which now concentrates on humanistic studies, and the other on mathematics and science. The two faculties award separate degrees which are designated as the Doctor of Philosophy I and the Doctor of Philosophy II, respectively. In most European universities, however, the philosophical conflict was ignored, and the scientific studies were accommodated by merely adding new chairs in the traditional faculties of philosophy.

Secondary education did not remain unchanged by the growing interest in scientific and technical studies. The appearance of technicums and polytechnical institutes to foster such studies encouraged politically important commercial cities to petition for accreditation of their municipal secondary schools. Denied the privilege of offering instruction in Latin when the system of state *Gymnasien* was created by royal decree, these municipal schools had been forced to limit instruction to the mother tongue, modern foreign languages, mathematics, elements of the new sciences, and other studies that were thought to have a practical as distinguished from an intellectual character. These subjects were called the *Realen*, a term which suggests, but is not identical with the English words "real" and "realism." The schools in which such studies were pursued came to be known as the *Realschulen*, but in contrast to the *Gymnasien*, their students could not be admitted to the maturity examinations, and hence they were also excluded from the universities, the professions, the civil service, and the officer ranks in the armed forces.

The patrons of the *Realschulen*, members of the new industrial and commercial classes, now argued that their schools offered the best possible preparation for successful studies in the technicums and polytechnical institutes. After prolonged negotiations, a second type of maturity examination was authorized by the government of Kaiser Wilhelm II that extended the privilege of admission to the technical institutes to students who had received their preparatory training in the accredited *Realschulen*. The new maturity examination was based upon modern languages, mathematics, and sciences, but no Latin.

The exclusion of Latin and Greek from the new examination indicated that the *Junker* aristocracy was not about to relax its monopolistic control over university admissions. Nevertheless, that monopoly was forced, in time, by the continuing upward thrust of the new classes residing in the cities. Helped by the rapidly expanding need for military surgeons for the imperial army and navy and for scientists (as distinguished from technicians) to promote the search for new knowledge, the patrons of some of the better *Realschulen* refuted the argument that a knowledge of Greek was necessary to succeed in either the study of medicine or the scientific departments of the faculties of philosophy. Hence, a third type of maturity examination was requested in which Latin was to be included, but modern languages were substituted for Greek. This form of examination was approved shortly before World War I and a few *Realschulen* were permitted to add Latin studies – but not Greek – to their curriculum. These schools became known as the *Realgymnasien*; to their graduates who succeeded in passing the designated maturity examination was extended the privilege of admission to the medical faculties and to the scientific departments of the faculties of philosophy – a privilege that was bitterly opposed by the *Gymnasien* and the faculties of philosophy.

Reforms Since World War II

The controversies over expanding universities by adding scientific studies, as well as over the two new types of maturity examinations, were still raging when World War I brought an end to the German Empire. The period of nominal peace between World War I and World War II provided little opportunity for the academic communities to do more than rebuild what had been destroyed. World War II proved even more destructive, but this time the efforts to rebuild received substantial assistance from abroad. Nevertheless, the reconstruction efforts to 1950 seem now to have been more concerned with restoring the university foundations as they had existed in 1914 than with instituting reforms designed to provide new answers to new problems. That is to say, states that survived the war as political entities restored their universities by reestablishing the traditional four professional faculties and reinstituted the traditional system of maturity examinations to regulate university admissions.

The traditional preparatory schools were also restored and reopened. In the German states, including Austria and the German-speaking cantons of Switzerland, the three types of preparatory schools and maturity examinations developed in the German Empire immediately prior to World War I are now all known as *Gymnasien*, but are differentiated by type as the "classical languages" *Gymnasien*, the "modern languages" *Gymnasien*, and the "mathematics-natural sciences" *Gymnasien*. Each typically is a separate school housed in its own quarters. Each receives its students from either the fourth or the sixth year of the elementary school, depending upon the region. Each sends its graduates to a separate branch of higher education, and young children, therefore, are still required to make their life commitment at the age of eleven or twelve, when the choice of which preparatory or continuation school they will enter is thrust upon them. Only since 1950 have significant changes in these matters been made.

Expanding the Role of the Universities

To appreciate the revolutionary nature of the reforms now taking place in European higher education, we must note that until about 1950 a university typically endeavored to cultivate a single philosophical and social outlook. The accepted world-view, or *Weltanschauung*, was that which we have chosen to call rational humanism. The universities drew their students from preparatory schools that planted the necessary intellectual seeds and carefully pruned and cultivated the young sprouts to assure that growth occurred only in the approved direction. The maturity examinations were used to determine if, and when, the young scholar was ready to be transplanted to the open fields of the university. Universities, in their turn, gave each young candidate for the learned professions the specialized tools appropriate to his chosen field of endeavor. But whether he chose law, medicine, philosophy, or theology he emerged from his studies with his basic world view unchanged and fully aware of the exclusive social class into which he was born and to which he still belonged.

In this rigidly structured academic establishment, the faculty of philosophy played the dominant role; Goethe was its hero. The most obvious product of university studies, therefore, was an intellectual like-mindedness which pervaded every section of the academic community.

It is also necessary for Americans to remember that the European university does not have, and never has had, a graduate school (such as is known here) within which the whole range of scholarly inquiry is accommodated under a single administrative head. In Europe, each faculty receives its students from the same general source. The accredited preparatory schools supposedly assure uniform backgrounds and aptitude. Those who enter the faculties of law, train as lawyers and generally become civil servants. The faculties of medicine produce physicians, dentists, pharmacists, and veterinarians. The faculties of theology produce theologians and clergymen. And the faculties of philosophy supply teachers for the preparatory schools and the future professors of philosophy. Each faculty supervises its own program and examines its own candidates for its own degrees.

This administrative structure quite obviously – at least to American eyes – has a built-in capacity for encouraging intellectual inbreeding, a disposition to resist ideas that do not conform to the established pattern of thought and action. Because faculties of philosophy are the exclusive sources of secondary school teachers, as well as for replacements for their own faculties, they have been able to maintain the rational humanistic tradition for nearly two hundred years. In France the faculties of philosophy prepare and administer the *Baccalaureat* examinations, and have thereby controlled not only admissions to all other faculties, but also the curriculum of the *lycées* and *collèges*, which are the only secondary schools that have enjoyed preparatory status.

Faculties of philosophy are now being told, however, that the power and prestige they have enjoyed for so long entails some rather weighty social responsibilities. In the troubled times that have followed World War II, many Europeans ask why their vaunted academic establishments offered no bulwark against Prussian autocracy between 1848 and 1914, the Nazi horror before World War II, or the two World Wars themselves. Some even ask why the university leadership, following each of these catastrophies, sought to lead men's minds back to the patterns of thought that dominated the last half of the nineteenth century.

As a consequence of such questioning, alternatives to the rational humanism are now being sought, not only outside the universities but increasingly within the university faculties themselves. Dialectical materialism is one such excursion into the philosophical unknown, existentialism is another. Whatever reservations we may have about each of these alternatives, the prospects are that the philosophical uniformity maintained in the universities for so long is now likely to be absent from the European scene for some time to come.

Evidence of the diminishing control exercised by the faculties of philosophy is found in the number of new faculties which now operate side-by-side with the traditional four. The faculty of mathematics and natural sciences is perhaps the most prominent of these. Sometimes called Philosophy II with authority to award the Doctor of Philosophy II degree, as at the University of Bern, these faculties of mathematics and natural sciences are showing a disposition to award the Doctor of Science degree. Some universities now also have a faculty of the social sciences, or of political science and economics. Some even have faculties of the applied sciences such as agriculture, architecture, commerce, engineering, and education. These newer fields of study, however, are still more likely to be found in attached but separate institutes and colleges. But whether incorporated as a faculty or attached as an institute, the new fields of study now generally enjoy university status. Many are authorized to conduct their own degree examinations, and to award their own degrees including the doctorate.

As a consequence of such expansion into new fields of inquiry, the universities are rapidly losing their air of detachment from the cares of the world about them. Students enrolled in a faculty of philosophy, of science, or of the social sciences who are anticipating a career as teachers must now attach themselves to a university institute or department of education. There they will receive specialized instruction in psychology and methodology, and be given opportunities to observe teaching and to acquire supervised practice in teaching. Other specialized institutes and centers established in connection with universities afford similar opportunities for practical experiences and advanced training, particularly in applied research. Indeed, it is now becoming increasingly difficult to distinguish between universities and polytechnical institutes on the basis of their involvement in either pure research or the application of knowledge in solving the specific problems that arise out of the everyday experiences of the society that supports them.

A final observation regarding the new role of universities reflects the changing character of the student bodies. World War II and the reconstruction years that followed seem to have had a revolutionary effect on the rigidly class-structured societies from which the students come. Prior to those disturbing events, it was thought that one must be born to the class for which opportunities in higher education are designed in order to be permitted to take advantage of them. Those not so favored by their Creator learned to know their subordinate places early in life and seldom struggled to rise above their designated class by demanding an education normally reserved to their superiors. This selective factor assured the universities that their students could afford to attend on a full-time basis; and an individual who did not possess the necessary personal resources, or the leisure, simply did not matriculate.

Academic snobbishness, though still present, is now rapidly giving way to a more open attitude. Fully qualified students increasingly sign up for only a few of the lectures normally offered in a given semester or term. They may even support themselves by part-time or full-time employment. Evening courses are being instituted by the universities and other institutions of higher education to accommodate such part-time study. The newer faculties and departments have been particularly cooperative in these matters, as have the technical and other specialized schools and institutes.

In England, where part-time study has recently come to enjoy great popularity, only 15,000 full-time students were enrolled in the 762 establishments of higher education in 1959-60, whereas 79,000 were enrolled on a part-time basis.[4] The number of part-time students was larger than the combined enrollments of the conventional universities. Twenty-four percent of the degrees granted by the University of London in that same year were awarded to individuals who had not been regularly enrolled but had prepared themselves for the degree examinations. Six percent of the first degrees awarded by all universities in England and Wales in 1959-60 were "external" degrees.[5]

Such involvement of the universities in upgrading the general population through programs of continuing and part-time education is now growing, not only in the British Isles, but on the

---

[4] J. A. Lauwerys, "United Kingdom: England and Wales," *Access to Higher Education* (Paris: UNESCO, 1965), II, 508.

[5] *Ibid.*, p. 515.

Continent as well. The effect of this trend on the traditional, highly selective preparatory schools, and on the equally traditional university admissions procedures, thus merits special notice.

Reforming Preparatory Studies

The nature of the changes presently occurring in European higher education were forecast by reforms that occurred in secondary education. While the humanistic curriculum is still very much in evidence and, in the oldest and most exclusive secondary schools has scarcely been changed from the form given it by the Prussians around 1850, the upward thrust of the working classes since World War II has broken the monopoly these schools once enjoyed. The tuition rates that all preparatory schools formerly charged (thereby restricting opportunities to prepare for university studies to the highest socio-economic classes) either have been mitigated by scholarships and grants-in-aid, or eliminated entirely. In Switzerland, for example, this trend was started in Zurich less than ten years ago by one individual who initiated a popular referendum on the tuition issue. The subsequent popular vote to abandon tuitions in all public secondary schools carried overwhelmingly in spite of official opposition. Similar action has since been taken in nearly all the other cities and cantons of Switzerland that operate public secondary schools.

The English Education Act of 1944 was originally aimed at equalizing educational opportunities through a system of grants-in-aid to the able but needy scholars. Today, public policy is emphasizing the building of new institutions in such numbers and locations that opportunity to attend is freely accessible to all who wish further education. In France the local (and therefore more accessible) municipal *collèges* have now been made equal with the state *lycées* in both financial support and the access to higher studies they afford their students. The traditional tuition fees have been eliminated or soon will be.

Communist countries, in contrast, have always looked upon the student as one who is rendering an important public service for which he should be paid regular wages. However, the decision to attend school, even for those beyond the compulsory age level, is not for the student to make.

These efforts to broaden the socio-economic basis of the university populations have been related to program changes in the secondary schools. The fact that changes were needed was brought to light only very recently by the few, newly established institutes of sociology and other agencies for research in the social sciences. Since 1950, both government and industry have complained bitterly that the traditional preparatory schools and universities were failing to provide either the number or the quality of trained personnel needed to fill the managerial and supervisory positions that have developed in the postwar economy. The professions, including teaching, are equally troubled by recruitment problems in the face of the population explosion and the rising expectations of the middle and lower classes. A succession of manpower studies, most of which have appeared since 1960, predict that these crippling shortages will persist to at least 1975. The key to the recruitment problem, say Swiss government and educational leaders,[6] is to be found "on the steps of the secondary schools."

The Swiss viewpoint in this matter arises, in part, from the fact that for the European boy or girl the decision to continue his education beyond the level of the elementary school has had to be made at the age of eleven or twelve. The reason for this early decision was provided by the Prussians in a manner we have already described. That is to say, certain schools known in German regions as *Gymnasien* were made the sole avenue through which one could enter a university or qualify to practice a profession. The combined enrollments of these highly selective preparatory schools have seldom exceeded seven percent of the secondary school age population; and only about half of those admitted have been able to complete successfully the program of studies offered. That is to say, government, the professions, commerce and industry have had only four percent of the population supply their needs for academically trained personnel.

Many Europeans – and even a few unhappy Americans – have regarded the handful of young men and women who have qualified for university admission in the above manner as evidence of the European system's superior quality. They have said that only the intellectually gifted, the natural leaders in each generation, find their way into leadership positions when the portals to such positions are carefully guarded by a system of preparatory

---

[6] *Aktuelle Mittelschulfragen* (Zurich: Cantonal Department of Education, 1964), p. 5.

studies of such high quality. But European sociologists now question this easy assumption and offer data to support their claim that in the face of growing personnel shortages the system has wasted much of the human potential that has been available.

Recent studies show that in Switzerland two of three children reaching age eleven or twelve (the age at which they must decide to transfer to a preparatory school offering foreign language instruction if they are later to go on to an institution of higher education) elect to continue in a vernacular school. This choice, it has been found, is more closely related to the father's vocation and the level of family income than to the pupil's predicted academic potential.[7] Studies of the socio-economic backgrounds of students enrolled in Swiss universities show that over sixty percent come from families in which the father is a professional man or is self-employed. In contrast, only about three percent come from families where the father is employed in a manual occupation in either agriculture or industry.[8]

Suspicious that university enrollments also reflect geographic as well as social discrimination, in 1964 Professor Meili of the University of Bern administered a special academic aptitude test to a carefully drawn sample of Swiss children. The average age of the 1842 children tested was eleven years and six months. The sample included a fair representation from the major geo-economic regions ranging from the commercial cities to the rural highlands; and the major socio-economic classes ranging from the professional and self-employed to the day laborers. Professor Meili concluded from his data that talent is rather evenly distributed among the various regions and social classes, but that the lack of stimulating experiences and cultural opportunities in certain communities does not encourage such talent to develop. He suggested that the lack of appropriate educational opportunities in rural highland regions is one form of such cultural limitation.

Since 1960 two rather marked developments have occurred in Swiss secondary education that indicate a trend which is becoming

---

[7]Pierre Oguey. "Des moyens d'etendre le recrutement de l'Universite et de faciliter l'accès des études supérieures." *Archiv für das Schweizerische Unterrichtswesen* (Frauenfeld: Verlag Huber & Co., 1959), Vol. 45, 71; Willi Schneider. "Sociologische Untersuchungen uber Basler Schulprobleme," *Basler Schulblatt*, Vol. 25, No. 3 (May 1964), p. 72.

[8]Oguey, *op. cit.*, 74-75.

common to much of Western Europe. The first development would make it possible for all children to delay the decision as to which educational track they will pursue until after they have completed their sixth year of elementary schooling. Since children in Northern Europe normally do not begin their elementary schooling until the age of seven, this rather crucial educational and vocational decision could thus be delayed until age thirteen or later. In recognition of this change, the study of Latin is not to be introduced in any school until the child's seventh school year. The effect is to keep the door to the several preparatory programs open to children from the suburban and rural areas who ordinarily must either commute to the city from their homes or arrange to live with relatives if they are to receive a preparatory education.

The second development is seen in a trend toward the comprehensive secondary school and the offering of a limited number of elective subjects to replace the present rigid, single-tract program of required subjects. In France, and in the French-speaking cantons of Switzerland, the trend is to terminate elementary education at the end of the sixth year and to require all pupils completing the sixth year to enter a comprehensive secondary school. The initial part of this common secondary school program (a period which may last as long as two years for some pupils) is looked upon as a period of observation for purposes of guidance. On an experimental basis, pupils elect to enter one of the three parallel programs offered. Opportunities to transfer from one program to another are provided as late as in the eighth school year; and even those who elect the practical program may study Latin on an optional basis. This flexibility has the advantage of delaying the final choice of an educational career until age fourteen or fifteen.

Several experimental schools, such as the municipal *Gymnasien* at Thun (also in Switzerland) defer the beginning of Latin until the ninth or even the tenth school year. This arrangement is designed to permit pupils, particularly those in rural areas, to complete their studies in a vernacular elementary or secondary school, and thus to enter the university preparatory program—that is, to begin studying Latin—at what is for Europeans a very late age.

While the developments in Switzerland are admittedly coming more rapidly than in many of the neighboring states, due to the Swiss level of prosperity and the decentralized form of administrative authority, all countries of Europe are now seeking to extend educational opportunity through the reorganization of their systems of secondary education. As a consequence, some children now attending academic secondary schools come from families in which no member has ever received an education beyond the minimum prescribed by law. A few such students will soon find their way into the universities; and thence into the professions. A larger number will seek specialized training in science and the technologies.

This upward flow from the lower socio-economic groups is increasing rapidly, and universities already are beginning to cope with the new problems their expanded enrollments are thrusting upon them. The solution is not merely to build more universities, although the number is likely to double in the very near future, but to develop new types of universities to serve the modern needs. In this connection it is a rather startling experience to witness the phenomenal popularity the English colleges of advanced technology have earned within the last decade. In Switzerland, it is the National Technical University in Zurich that has caught the public eye and is now being imitated at Aarau, Lausanne, and Luzern.

But even in the traditional universities, the administrative authorities are now beginning to be concerned with the need to provide academic counseling, to supervise the social life of the students, and even to provide them suitable housing and food and health services. As a consequence, some of the "red brick" campuses may soon bear much more than a mere physical resemblance to their numerous counterparts on this side of the Atlantic.

Liberalizing the Admissions Procedures

Reference was made earlier to the role played by the maturity examinations in promoting and perpetuating the academic tradition initiated by the Prussians during the first half of the nineteenth century. It will be recalled that a civil authority known as the *Schulkollegium* was established by the Prussians to administer the examinations. The charge given these provincial authorities was to make certain that nobody proceeded from a secondary school to a university who did not have the necessary maturity to cope with the stipulated academic fare. It was understood that competency in both Latin and Greek was necessary to assure such success. Greek later was made optional, but only at the price of a greater emphasis on Latin studies and the addition of modern foreign languages and the mother tongue.

Protected by the barricade the maturity examinations afforded them, universities enjoyed the privilege of continuing in their traditional ways, comfortable in the knowledge that all their students had a high level of language facility, and a humanistic philosophical orientation.

Current efforts to broaden the flow of students entering the universities are often directed against the maturity system. Such efforts have already produced new types of university admissions certificates, particularly in the German states. In addition to the traditional Type A certificate, which attests to a mastery of Greek and Latin, and the Type B certificate, which bears witness to a mastery of Latin and the modern languages, the Type C or mathematics, science, and modern languages certificate also has been declared valid in certain university faculties. In both Switzerland and West Germany, scientific and technical studies have gained academic status equal to that of philosophy and the older professional faculties. Indeed, the need for many more physicians, dentists, veterinarians, pharmacists, and other medical scientists has brought about a bitter debate over whether competency in Latin shall continue to be a requirement for admission to medical studies. In Switzerland, a national commission of experts appointed to study this matter has already recommended making Latin optional, thus making it possible for anyone holding a Type C certificate to be admitted into a medical faculty and ultimately to the examination for a federal certificate to practice medicine.

But breaking the Latin monopoly is not the end of the present battle to reform admissions policies. The rise of faculties of the social and commercial sciences has already produced vigorous support for a new maturity certificate, tentatively identified as the Type H certificate. A few venturesome municipalities and other school patrons have already instituted maturity programs based on modern languages and the social sciences. The programs have been either added to existing commercial or other type of secondary schools, or organized as independent institutions. Equally courageous universities are accepting the students from such schools on the basis of the still unaccredited Type H certificate.

Experiments are also underway with modern foreign language programs. The certificate that marks the successful completion of such a program is tentatively designated as Type D. In West Germany, several communities are reported to be experimenting with a program that combines music and the humanities. All these, and other programs not mentioned here, have been designed on the assumption that languages and literature are not the only disciplines that mature the intellectual powers, a claim for which the proponents of such programs now offer some rather convincing supporting evidence.

A less revolutionary but increasingly popular innovation is the so-called *Zweite Bildungsweg*, literally the second way to acquire an education. It is an arrangement that provides the traditional preparatory programs leading to the traditional maturity examinations to individuals who were not able to complete their preparatory studies in the conventional way. The "second way" is open to adults only, usually on a part-time basis, and in an abbreviated form. The agencies providing such instructions have therefore become known as "evening *Gymnasien*."

The revolutionary character of the "second way" is evidenced by the fact that the program may be completed in about three and one-half years. This is in sharp contrast to the six years traditionally regarded as the absolute minimum for the proper maturation of boys and girls attending the regular day schools. The latter, or conventional, way is still the preferred way, however, and the school authorities have clearly stated that the "second way" is reserved to adults who have already been licensed for a recognized trade or vocation and have successfully practiced that occupation for a specified number of years. It is interesting that the "second way" leads almost without exception to either a Type A or a Type B maturity examination.

These experiments with newer programs and examinations, as well as with other aspects of the university admissions procedures, are possible because there is now a trend in all of Europe toward decentralization of authority in secondary as well as in higher education. This trend is particularly evident in the universities of Switzerland and West Germany, but the movement toward centralized control that appeared in postwar England is now also beginning to reverse itself. And in France the faculties of philosophy must now share their control over the admissions examinations with teachers in the secondary schools.

The liberalizing trends are more evident in Switzerland and West Germany because the universities in these places are agencies of the cantons, or of the states, as distinguished from the national governments. As such, they are more immediately responsive to the public they serve than are the national universities in neighboring lands. It follows that the agencies in charge of the maturity examinations are also closer to the people with the result that local variations in examination standards and practices no longer provide the uniformity of instruction that once prevailed in both secondary schools and the universities. Examples of such local variations can again be taken from Switzerland.

The Swiss had established a federal maturity commission late in the nineteenth century to bring about uniformity in the several universities as a basis for issuing federal licenses to practice. The cantons, however, had enjoyed sovereign rights in education for centuries and were not disposed to let a federal agency usurp any of their privileges. The federal maturity commission was therefore forced to limit its regulatory efforts to prescribing requirements for admission to examinations on the basis of which a federal license to practice medicine would be issued. One of the requirements the federal commission prescribed for admission to the examinations was a Type A or Type B maturity certificate issued by a federally accredited maturity school. The federal maturity commission then published a list of those schools which, in its judgment, offered acceptable programs of instruction and whose certificates of maturity would be accepted for admission to the federal medical examinations.

This compromise between the federal maturity commission and the cantonal educational authorities had the effect of leaving the schools and universities, as well as the maturity examinations themselves, in the hands of the respective cantons. Indeed, each canton continued to be free to establish and operate any school and to institute any programs it found desirable and to issue whatever certificates or diplomas it thought appropriate in each case. The cantonal universities, including the medical faculties, were also free to admit students on the basis of the maturity certificates accredited by the cantons in addition to those accredited by the federal commission; and the cantons could continue issuing licenses to practice the medical professions. Such cantonal certificates would be valid, of course, within the issuing cantons only.

Having reasserted their sovereignty, the cantons tended to rest easy and to accept the standard set by the federal commission as the standards for their own maturity certificates. Indeed, the number of maturity certificates issued by the cantons decreased substantially, and the federal commission was so generally accepted as a beneficial influence in education that its current regulations, issued in 1925, were not seriously questioned until about 1950. Because the great depression and World War II produced a surplus of trained personnel in all fields, the federal maturity commission continued to insist upon a maturity certificate based on Latin studies–that is, either a Type A or Type B certificate–for admission to the medical examinations. The other university faculties, supported by the respective professional associations, were also disposed to limit admissions to holders of these two types of certificates.

The economic and social situation since 1950 has not been one to tolerate an educational policy that had hardened into tradition under vastly different circumstances. The professions as well as commerce and industry are now crying for many more trained recruits. Administrative specialists as well as scientists and technicians are needed in large numbers. The proponents of these newer fields are not disposed to permit the Latin teachers to determine who may take up the studies that prepare for these newer specialties. Even the medical profession is now about to accept the abolition of Latin as a required subject for admission to the practice of medicine, and nearly all medical faculties have already admitted students who meet the existing Latin requirement merely by passing a deficiency examination administered by the universities themselves. The degree of mastery required obviously may vary substantially from university to university and from year to year.

The authority of the federal maturity commission to influence instruction on the secondary level is now challenged on the ground that its regulations allow wide variations in their enforcement. It must be understood in this connection that the Swiss Federal Maturity Commission does not prepare and administer the maturity examinations; nor does it evaluate the papers written by the students. The Commission merely accredits individual schools which may then examine their own students and issue a maturity certificate bearing the stamp of federal approval to those of its students who, in the school's judgment, have successfully passed the local examination. In recent years, accredited schools have also been allowed to consider the student's course marks in determining who shall be awarded a maturity certificate.

It follows that considerable variation is now apparent in the degree of difficulty students experience in the examinations at the various maturity schools. A gross example is found in the case of the cloister school at Einsedeln which does not think its students—all boys—are ready for their examinations before age twenty-one or twenty-two, and does not issue certificates except to students who have demonstrated a mastery of Latin. In contrast, the minimum age at the Zurich cantonal *Gymnasium* is eighteen as it is elsewhere, and many certificates of Type C (without Latin) are issued each year. Since the Type A and Type B certificates from either school are accepted as equivalent by any Swiss university, it follows that the prudent student from a nonaccredited school desiring a federally approved maturity certificate will take his maturity examination at Zurich instead of Einsedeln.

But the revolt against regulation by a central educational agency has lately taken a more radical turn. Cantonal departments of education under pressure from parents seeking expanded opportunities for their children, and from commerce and industry asking for many more persons with some academic training in the physical and social sciences as well as in the technical fields, are responding by determining their own standards for admission to their cantonal universities as well as for graduation from their secondary schools. Cantonal maturity certificates are again being issued, and in rapidly increasing numbers, by both federally accredited and non-accredited schools. The cantonal universities are admitting the holders of such certificates, particularly into the faculties that offer training in the newer administrative and managerial specialties. In August of 1964, the Canton of Zurich even threatened to admit students without Latin into the Medical faculty of the University of Zurich; and to issue its own licenses to practice the medical professions within the limits of the canton or of any other canton that may decide to accept the Zurich licenses. This is nothing short of a declaration of academic independence, and an announcement that from now on the Canton of Zurich will develop and operate its own programs of higher secondary education as it sees fit.

Somewhat quieter declarations of independent action have come from Basel and Bern. Besieged by a shortage of graduates from the conventional programs of theological studies that has resulted in being unable to staff the established church with conventionally trained clergymen, these cantons have very recently introduced crash programs open to persons who lack the normal qualifications for admission to the theological faculties. In Bern, an intensive short course in the elements of Latin and Greek has now been introduced to prepare adults for admission to its faculty of theology. The course of theological studies has also been shortened, but is supplemented by a year of internship in a parish under the direction of the regular pastor. Following the successful completion of the internship, the graduate of this special program is declared eligible for election to a pastorate of his own on a basis equal to that of candidates who have completed the conventional program of theological studies. The authorities in Basel have instituted a post-secondary, but sub-university, theological seminary that offers a short and more practical training for the clergy than does the conventional faculty of theology.

Meanwhile, the Federal Polytechnical Institute at Zurich has achieved university status and the Institute for Commercial and Social Sciences at St. Gallen is about to do so. Each readily accepts students on the basis of a cantonal maturity certificate in addition to those who have federally accredited certificates. Higher technical schools are not only rapidly increasing in numbers and expanding their offerings, but are being upgraded so that most now award federally accredited diplomas in at least some of their programs. The diplomas are roughly the equivalent of an American bachelor's degree in engineering or in business administration.

The Swiss developments in higher education have their counterparts throughout most of northern Europe. The speed with which the innovations have appeared varies from country to country and inversely with the degree of administrative control that is exercised in education by the central government. This is true even in the Soviet Union, for once the Communists had imposed their sweeping reforms shortly after the Revolution, the dead weight of a massive bureaucracy has impeded subsequent change on any significant scale.

Summarizing briefly, any American who wishes to understand higher education in Europe today must be prepared to find universities that excpect their students to have completed their general education before they are admitted and to be ready to concentrate upon a relatively narrow field of specialized professional studies. Each field is under the supervision of its own faculty that controls not merely the program of instruction, but the degree requirements as well. Thus, the program in the faculty of philosophy in a given university is normally completed in three years, whereas a program in the faculty of medicine in the same university may require six years or even seven. The universities of continental Europe have neither a faculty of liberal arts nor a graduate school; and in many cases, as in France, do not even have a campus. In the latter case, the university is essentially an administrative agency that looks after all higher education provided in its designated geographical area. The rector is an official appointed by the central ministry of education. As a result of historical accident, the faculty of philosophy may be located in one town, the faculty of law in another, and the faculty of medicine in still a third. Members of one faculty seldom meet members of another or participate in a joint activity.

The popular concept of a university as a community of scholars working together in the pursuit of knowledge by similar means will be even more rudely shattered as the trend toward diversity of instruction and methods of research proliferates faculties and degrees, and invites a highly diversified body of students to partake of the increasingly extensive academic fare. Uniformity in philosophy or socio-economic origins is already a relic of the past. European universities have already been caught up in the headlong rush to achieve social change and, indeed, may soon reassert their original claim as seats of learning that rightfully afford intelligent direction to change itself. In this sense, it may be a moot question whether Americans should continue to look to European universities for guidance, or if the reverse is already in process.

Education in the Canadian Provinces

Neville V. Scarfe

The British-North America Act

In 1866, Canada became self-governing, independent, and unified under the title of the Dominion of Canada. The Mother of Parliaments in Westminster, England, enacted the famous British-North America Act, which not only set up a completely separate Parliament and self-governing organization in Ottawa, but also succeeded in uniting a huge continental mass with a great diversity of topography, natural resources, and people.

As is typical of most English legislation, the establishment of this new independent nation was a masterpiece of compromise. It succeeded in balancing all the conflicting forces, desires, and aspirations into some form of agreed harmony, with a willingness to coexist, cooperate, and collaborate; it included every form of toleration and protection for minorities and differing viewpoints. It should be emphasized that this legislation was a masterpiece because in those days, when there was no connecting link across Canada either by railway, road, air, or water, it was an enormous achievement to have secured unity in such tremendous diversity. Although an English government established this nation, every effort was made to protect the rights of the French minority. The British government was, by law, Anglican in religion, but it leaned over backward to protect religious minorities, whether Catholic, Lutheran, or other. In particular, the British-North America Act protected the rights of education, In fact, this law recognized diversity in Canada by setting up provinces, each with its own separate legislature, and each with its absolute control over the educational activities within that province. Full and complete control over all forms of education was vested solely with the provincial legislators, and these powers have been most jealously guarded and protected.

Such an arrangement was apparently good, useful, necessary, and important one hundred years ago, but with the numerous changes during the past century, ideas that were fruitful and important then are now open to question and doubt. Good schemes outlive their usefulness. One of the strange paradoxes of this educational arrangement is that it was based on the English idea that education was best managed by teachers. Perhaps we could express it in a slightly different way by saying that the British system delegated powers and responsibilities for education to the local authorities. The system assumed that parents and teachers, who make up a local community, know best what they want and need for their children. It was natural, therefore, and very obvious to English legislators that education should be delegated to the provinces, and they assumed that provincial governments, in their turn, would delegate powers and responsibilities to local school boards. This is, in fact, what had to happen one hundred years ago, simply because of the difficulty of communication and the wide scope and variety of needs.

Centralization of Educational Administration

Things did not work out in an English way; they worked out in a Canadian way. Canada is an enormous country with great distances and great diversities–it is not a small, crowded country where roads, railways, and canals develop readily, and where communication by sea is very simple. In England, it has always been very easy for the people to become uniform. Thus, they have always favored and encouraged diversity. In Canada, as it is much too easy to remain different and to become diverse, the Canadians had to encourage some forms of uniformity. The provincial governments never fully delegated their centralized powers. On the contrary, they tended to increase the centralization and accumulation of power within a few hands, and to take away from the small local communities their responsibilities for education.

No weapon was more effective in producing unity and conformity within diverse provincial environments than the earliest of all mass produced products–the school textbook. Schools were used, therefore (as within the United States in the early days), as political agents to unify the nation. Textbooks encouraged most people to speak English and learn English grammar, to have common vicarious experiences, common reading material, and common understandings. Similarly, the school system in the United States was the most effective of the early weapons in converting the United States into the great melting pot.

The Dominion of Canada was not, however, ever conceived as a melting pot. There was no insistence on everyone learning a common language, but there was still an urgent, if not a greater, need to unify the great diversity, for Canada is larger than the U.S.A.; it has greater distances east to west; it has greater distances north to south. Newfoundland differs more markedly from British Columbia than do the New England states from Washington and Oregon, or Florida from Texas or California. Similarly, the great contrasts between Ontario and the Northwest Territories are sharper than those between Chicago, Illinois, and Birmingham, Alabama. In a land larger than the United States, there exists only one-tenth of the population, and the problem of unifying French-speaking and English-speaking Canada is as great, or greater, than the problem of unifying Negro and white in the United States.

There is a trend, therefore, not only to concentrate and centralize educational opportunities in the provinces, but to unify education across Canada, even though each province still has an entirely separate educational system. All provinces tend to use similar textbooks and curricula, and each tries to organize interchangeability of teaching certificates. The provinces would like the central federal government to provide more and more financial support for education but without any control. Certainly, some aspects of centralization and mutual coordination promote efficiency and take care of the great mobility of population within our continent.

It is not the educators, however, who are producing unification and centralization; it is being brought about by forces external to education. Although textbooks were the earliest of the standardized products in this era of mass production, industry has now produced a tremendous number of other standardized products. We find the same types of automobiles, refrigerators, frozen vegetables, and television sets all over North America. The speed of communication, distribution of products, mobility of people, instantaneous transmission of news and ideas have encouraged uniformity throughout the whole of this area so that today the great danger of our civilization is mass uniformity. The educational system alone is not responsible for this standardization–the revolts in our universities are also directed against society's impersonalization of human beings. "Inhuman" machines and overcrowding of our cities tend to develop a mass mediocracy. Thus, schools have suddenly found themselves with an entirely different function. Instead of being the main medium for unifying the nation, they are now the main means by which we can encourage diversity and individualism.

It is partly because of the modern tendency to unification, integration, and centralization that there exists a conflict between the separatists in Quebec and the unifiers in the rest of Canada. There is obviously economic advantage in centralized planning and economic collaboration, and much efficiency in the mechanization and specialization of industry. Petty politics of local communities and ignorant provincialism are avoided when education is nationally organized.

There are many aspects of education, however, and many aspects of human life that do not lend themselves to the mechanical, monolithic, or "business efficiency" outlook. Some forms of educational administration can be computerized, and there are great advantages in easy, rapid exchange of information and data. On the other hand, there are important elements described under the increasingly vague terms "creative" or "divergent" or "human" that are destroyed by excessive centralization. There has to be some form of compromise between ruthless efficiency and human frailty, between uniformity and diversity, and between the useful planning of a welfare state and the ingenious discoveries of free enterprise. Educators and politicians are, therefore, at variance over the disposition of educational power.

Compromise

Compromise is much more characteristic of Canada than of the United States. This is due as much to force of circumstances as it is to environmental needs. In education, two major influences have affected the Canadian educational system. These are the influences of the English motherland, or the "old country" as it is called, and the influences of Canada's neighbor in the New World–the United States. In the old days, the influence of the English system was greater. In modern times, because there can be no barriers to television or radio and because the border is the freest in the world, the influence of the United States has been greater.

There are still many, however, who feel that the freedom of the English teacher from authoritarian controls is healthy and desirable, Many Canadians and English still explain that the Minister of Education in the central government of Great Britain has powers only to issue "suggestions for the consideration of teachers." Inspectors of schools have no powers over the teachers in an English school; they act through kindly advice and fruitful suggestions. On the other hand, the Canadian school system avoids the traditional elitism of the English private school or the discriminative selectiveness of the English grammar school.

It is interesting to note in passing that the tendency in Canadian education is to adopt the curriculum changes suggested by the United States. Many of the textbooks used in Canada are produced in the United States, or they are modifications of those in use in the United States. The great contribution that the United States has made to education is the constant improvement of the curriculum by bringing it up to date with modern knowledge. We must also appreciate that in the United States there is a close articulation between the world of work outside the classroom and activities within the classroom.

The improvements in *methods* of teaching, however, as adopted in Canada are derived from the English-training colleges and schools of education. (One of the great retarding factors in French-speaking Quebec has been the failure to forsake the old-fashioned, rigid, memoritor methods of the French teaching system.)

Indigenous Canadianism

It would be possible to show a great number of ways in which Canadians have adopted a compromise between American and English philosophies in their education. But perhaps today we should confine our discussion to the things that are distinctly Canadian and to examine these in somewhat greater detail. As already mentioned, one of the special and distinctive characteristics of Canadian education is the unified control vested in each province and the complete powers given to each provincial Minister of Education. Added to this is the total absence of any governmental organization in the Federal Parliament dealing with education.

Federal Activities

Of course, in Canada, the strange anomaly is that the federal government does play an indirect part in certain aspects of education. Until recently, the federal government provided some assistance to universities both in their operating and capital finances. The federal government also takes care of education within the armed forces. Through its Ministry of Labour, it is able to accomplish a certain amount of retraining of workers by encouraging vocational and technical training wherever such activities transcend provincial barriers. The Department of Northern Affairs is responsible for the education of Eskimos and Indians. Through the National Research Council, the federal government has assisted scientific research in universities; and the Medical Research Council has assisted similar activities in medicine. Nevertheless, the federal government has never been able to provide research funds for professional education; it has not been able to interfere with, or make grants to any educational activity under the control of the provincial Minister of Education.

One strange occurrence in recent months has been the attempt of the ten Ministers of Education to set up an interprovincial board or committee of education with the object of securing funds from the federal government in dealing with problems specifically Canadian. It is interesting to see the provincial Ministers of Education jealously guarding their provincial rights, yet wanting to set up an interprovincial, not federal, central office of education. The situation is further confused because very recently the federal government decided to give up its attempt to earmark specific grants even for universities through provincial governments. Instead, it now prefers to make a block grant to provinces of monies they may use as they like. Universities, of course, are appalled at this. They were much happier to get the impartial formula grant from the federal government than to be subjected to the petty politics of provincial legislatures, with their tempermental politicians.

Provincial Education

In most provinces, the local legislature has enacted laws to control the structure of the school system, to compel attendance at school from the age of six to fifteen or sixteen, to authorize building standards, to regulate teachers' qualifications, to stipulate textbooks, to allocate funds, and to prescribe the curriculum. While the provincial governments do not prescribe the methods of teaching, nevertheless, through its system of external examinations, most provinces exercise considerable control over what is taught and how it is taught. In each province there continues to be much conflict between the central authority of the Minister and the local authorities represented by the school boards. In addition, there is considerable conflict between the teachers' associations or unions and both the school boards and the provincial governments. There may be additional conflicts set up by parent-teacher organizations, and it is not unusual for chambers of commerce, or other business organizations within the community to interfere in, or to criticize the school system.

Royal Commissions

The result is that education is constantly in ferment, and it is not surprising that in the last decade there have been six provincial Royal Commissions investigating education. Provincial legislatures are conservative bodies just as are local school boards. They have been elected by taxpayers to keep down the taxes. Royal Commissions, appointed by conservative bodies, tend to be somewhat conservative and therefore they are unlikely to recommend revolutionary changes. Their tendency is to reconfirm most of what has proved to be traditionally good and to tinker with certain modifications that might remove the most obvious grievances or errors. In general, members of these commissions are terrified of anything that might be called "progressive education," and so they adhere rather strictly to the formal, the academic, the rigorous, the demanding hard-core subjects of the curriculum and have reinforced this by a system of external examinations on which entry to a university depends.

Royal Commissions have tended to shy away from any root-and-branch change in traditional schooling. They have addressed themselves instead to less controversial issues such as the equalization of educational opportunities between rural and urban areas, and the problem of providing for the enormously increased numbers of students attending high school. In this connection, the commissions have made an attempt to liberalize the old-fashioned academic programs that prepared scholars for the university. Instead, they have provided alternatives to the academic university entrance program. For those high school students who wish to enter business, industry, and commerce they have provided technical or vocational courses, shop work, secretarial practice, home economics, and the performing arts. It is clear that some children have no interest or aptitude for the formal academic subjects, that business and industry require skilled technicians and manual workers, and that service trades are increasing. And so the high schools, in various ways, have attempted to provide alternative courses.

Most of these efforts have failed because no amount of reorganization of an administrative structure, and no amount of tampering with the various programs can change the opinion of the general public that prestige attaches to the university entrance programs and that affluence results from these programs. The parents are not beguiled into thinking that such schemes are not discriminatory, segregative, or stereotyping. They want the academic program liberalized so that it interests all children.

Most of the Royal Commissioners have tended to emphasize intellectual training, and divided various subjects in the curriculum into the core, or hard subjects, and the peripheral, or frill subjects. The result is that in the high schools, tremendous prestige and emphasis is given to languages, science, and mathematics, whereas home economics, industrial arts, fine arts, music, and theatre are downgraded. Similarly, those who have special aptitudes in physical education and who can play on winning teams acquire prestige, but the less able have no significant form of physical fitness program.

In the 1960 report of the Royal Commission for the province of Manitoba, the following recommendations give the flavor of the conservative element animating some aspects of secondary education. The Commission recommended:

1. That school boards be authorized to prescribe, for boys and girls, at least some general standards of attire.
2. That the principal be required to *enforce* any regulations on attire of pupils issued by his school board.
3. That the principal be given adequate power to *enforce* any code of manners prescribed by his school board.
4. That the principal of each school be given the responsibility and authority to *enforce* reasonable discipline on the playground, in the lunchroom, and on the buses or vans transporting people to and from school.
5. In addition to their classroom duties, all teachers be *required* to be available for duty in some extra-curriculum activity for a period of two or three hours a week.
6. That teachers who are engaged in duties in or about the school be *required by regulation* to conduct themselves in such a way that sets a worthy example to their pupils.

Another quotation from their report reads as follows:

> The Commission believes it necessary to require in all grades, a core of academic subjects such as English, History, Geography, Mathematics, and the Sciences. Implicit in this insistence on a core of academic subjects is the necessity of securing a mastery of fundamentals. It is better for the pupil that he learn a few subjects well, than that he emerge with an unregistered mass of impressions of many subjects. To this end, the peripheral subjects permitted in any grade must be rigidly restricted to those that can be given in the time available, after satisfying the demand of the core subjects.

These regulations, in fact, seem not too different in intent or severity from that issued by the Ontario Government in 1872, which stated that:

> Any teacher who smokes, uses liquor in any form, frequents pool or public halls, or gets shaved in a barber shop, will give good reason to suspect his worth, intentions, integrity, and honesty.

It so happens that the province of Ontario still prescribes that the duty of teachers is to inculcate "by precept and example, sobriety, frugality, purity, temperance, and all other virtues."

In every province it is clearly stated that teachers can be suspended for disturbing the moral tone of the school. In Toronto, teachers are still forbidden to discuss in class those questions purely political or ecclesiastical or theological. Teachers are forbidden to express opinions adverse to British institutions or sentiments disloyal to the crown. In six provinces, departmental regulations govern everything from pictures and globes to brooms, thermometers, and toilets.

Where there has been a de-emphasis in the use of the IQ for the classification of students, the comprehensive, coeducational heterogeneous school and class organization has been broken down by various forms of streamlining—for example, the provision of classes for the retarded, and the adoption of what are called "major work" classes.

Progressive Movements

Counterbalancing these conservative tendencies, there has been a great upsurge in the improvement of teacher education across Canada. The Faculties of Education and Teachers Colleges have been the great liberalizing agents in encouraging more humane and up-to-date attitudes in education and in relating the rapid changes in society to similar necessary changes in the schools. The influence of professors of education on teachers has resulted primarily in improving methods of teaching. Thus, programmed learning, team teaching, the use of film and television, and the changing types of school buildings have resulted from the influence which professors of education and teachers have had on the provincial organizations.

In the opinion of many people, these changes have been too slow. One of the great retarding forces has been the shortage of teachers because it has encouraged Departments of Education and Ministers of Education to provide crash programs or watered-down courses for the training and education of teachers.

Improvements in education have been much more noticeable in the elementary than in the secondary schools. One of the most encouraging features of Canadian education is the increasing emphasis on preschool and kindergarten education, and on the application of some of the more successful practices from the early childhood level to the intermediate level. The rigid division of the elementary school into grades is being broken down; the idea of continuous growth and development is finding much favor. The use of teams of teachers to work with children is also being promoted. Elementary teachers are given freedom to make modifications and to initiate changes.

In the secondary school, however, the influence of tradition is still very clear and has been reinforced by the universities. As in the United States, the universities exercise considerable influence by their admission standards.

Much of the conservatism on the Canadian scene is due to lack of money, or rather to the competition for the financial resources at the disposal of governments. In a huge country with an extremely severe winter and a large, icy north, it is extremely expensive to build lines of communication across the continent and into the remote areas. These must be provided, however, by the gross national product earned by only twenty million people. It is difficult for a small population in a new but potentially rich land to find money for every aspect of its economy.

Canada is also a land where opportunities await all young men and women. Therefore, there is great competition among the professions for the highly qualified. That is why the teaching profession has labored for many years under a shortage of teachers. Also, we have been drawing our teachers from a period of low birth rate to teach children in an era of high birth rate.

Perhaps the amazing thing about it all is the tremendous progress that has been made in spite of all the difficulties enumerated. It seems necessary, therefore, to make special comments about teacher education in the provinces of Canada.

Teacher Education

Teacher education is a provincial matter, and is the special responsibility of the Minister of Education in each province. Until the postwar period, almost all teacher education in Canada was conducted under the direct surveillance of the Minister of Education in normal schools. These institutions usually accepted persons who, because of poverty, were unable to proceed to a university, or because of their lack of competence were not able to qualify for university entrance. In almost all cases, they had completed a high school education, took one year of training at a normal school, and then went out to teach in the elementary and junior high schools of the various provinces. Many high school teachers were also trained this way, although there has been a tendency to require a university degree.

In addition to the normal schools, for a number of years teachers for high schools have been trained at universities in a one-year postgraduate teacher-training course. This type of training followed the old English pattern and was usually operated under the Faculty of Arts. Some universities were able to offer a master's degree in education for those who wished to pursue studies beyond the initial training year. Although these operations were limited, they did tend to provide an elite in the teaching profession. Thus, high school teachers were given a different type of certificate, paid at a different rate, and accorded a prestige above that of persons trained in the normal school system.

The revolt against this type of plan has been slow, but twenty years ago the province of Alberta decided to bring all teacher education into the university orbit. The normal schools were closed and teachers were admitted to a Faculty of Education on the university campus. Attendance was, however, segregated to some degree from the rest of the university in order to admit students to the Faculty of Education with less than the regular university admissions standard. Furthermore, some trainees were permitted to leave the university and teach with only one or two years of education. In Alberta, the Department of Education continued to exercise considerable control over the Faculty of Education. Slowly, however, the Department has relaxed its control; the university has absorbed the teachers much more fully into the university circle, and the new Faculty of Education building is in the center of the campus. It is now usual for young people to secure four years of university teacher education before going out to teach.

Ten years ago, the province of British Columbia also decided to bring all teacher education within the orbit of the university. In this case, a new Faculty of Education came immediately and completely under the full direction of the university. The Department of Education relinquished all control over the curriculum, staff appointments, and finances. All the Department retained was the awarding of certificates. This it does, however, on the recommendation of the university. Essentially, this means that all teachers must meet university entrance standards, must take all their arts and science courses in Faculties of Arts and Science, and must meet the same standards as others in the university to earn their degrees. In fact, the Faculty of Education in the University of British Columbia exacts higher standards in the award of its degree than do the Faculties of Arts or Science. No one who has a failing mark in his work in the Faculty of Arts and Science may be admitted to the Faculty of Education. Those who are rejected by the Faculty of Education have to go back to the Faculties of Arts or Science. This has resulted in the professional training of the teacher being placed on a level with the training of a doctor or lawyer or engineer. It has raised the standard of teacher qualification far above that of any other province in Canada.

In recent years, the provinces of Saskatchewan and Manitoba have decided to adopt somewhat similar schemes to those of British Columbia and Alberta, but nowhere is the Faculty of Education so much a part of the university and so little controlled by the provincial government as in British Columbia.

In Ontario, great efforts have been made recently to integrate the normal schools or teachers colleges with the universities. Unfortunately, not all the universities have been willing to accept this particular burden; furthermore, there is a great deal of money invested in buildings and so the old traditional system of segregating secondary from elementary teachers still prevails. Segregation is also evident in the teachers organizations, where there are two federations instead of one.

In Quebec, despite the recommendations of the recent Parent Royal Commission, many teachers still are trained in small classical colleges that are affiliated in a very loose fashion with the University of Montreal.

In the Maritime Provinces, many attempts have been made to integrate a teacher training and university institution into one major Atlantic Provinces unit. Nevertheless, normal schools still remain, although some of the universities have established the one-year teacher-training course for secondary teachers.

In Newfoundland, schools are organized by five different religious groups. Teacher training is all under the aegis of Memorial University, but with exceedingly complicated links between university training and the five separate divisions of the Department of Education.

National Organizations of Education

From time to time, efforts have been made to establish national education bodies. The Canadian Teachers' Federation, for instance, is a federation of provincial teachers' associations, but its powers are strictly limited and each province tends to guard jealously its rights and privileges. There is a Canadian School Trustees Association that loosely links the various trustees' organizations of the provinces. Even within the provinces, trustees' organizations are rather loose, amorphous groups as individual localities find it difficult to act on a common basis.

The Canadian Education Association has for many years acted in the capacity of a national clearing office for the Government of Canada in Ottawa. For instance, it helps exchange teachers from overseas to establish themselves in the various localities. Through scholarship funds, it organizes exchanges of teachers across Canada. It acts for Canada in the UNESCO National Committee and advises the government when delegations are sent to international education conferences.

The Canadian Education Association has been strangely ineffective, however, in coordinating provincial matters even though it is an organization set up by the separate Ministers of Education of the ten provinces of Canada. The Association is managed to a major degree by the Deputy Ministers of Education and by some of the Chief Superintendents, yet it has never had sufficient funds to do anything on a large scale. Moreover, funds for the Canadian Education Association are annually supplied from the various provincial coffers without any guarantee that they will continue during the subsequent year.

The professors of education in various universities of Canada have formed themselves into an association called the "Canadian Association of Professors of Education." This group meets once a year, along with the other learned societies of Canada and the Association of Universities of Canada.

Research

Research in education is almost wholly ignored by the provincial governments. Canada's richest province spends less than one-tenth of one percent of its total educational expenditure on research. Recently, this same province set up a special institute for studies in education. This institute is closely associated with the University of Toronto although not fully a part of that institution.

So far, no national body organized on a Canada-wide basis with support from the federal government has ever been formed to support education. There is an organization called the "Canada Council for Research in Education," but it is a small impoverished body unable to support research in any important way. Thus, in Canada research in professional education has progressed very slowly indeed.

From time to time, small sums of money have been granted by the W. K. Kellogg Foundation, the Imperial Oil Foundation, trustees' organizations, and even by teachers' organizations for the promotion of research. These have been small annual grants that do not permit any large scale scientific experiment or investigation into the problems of classroom learning.

Canadians, therefore, have to rely heavily on results of research undertaken in the United States and, to some extent, in European countries. It is in the field of educational research that the British-North America Act of a hundred years ago has its most deleterious effect. Although from time to time the federal government has been very favorably disposed to the setting up of an educational research council, the provinces have always turned their backs on this proposal, or at least one province has always rejected the suggestion, with the result that the other nine are not able to profit from such benefactions.

The Adolescent Revolt

At the present time, there is a great deal of discussion about education across the entire dominion. This has resulted primarily from the "revolt of the adolescent," or the revolt of the university student. The demands of youth to be heard in the councils of society are likely to result in great liberalization of the educational system of Canada.

For many years the effect of the sputnik was to give to the conservative, reactionary, and highly academic elements of society a marked influence on education. The Royal Commissions of Canada advocated a return to "the three r's" and to stricter discipline, more rigorous scholarship, and a greater emphasis on the sciences. Cultural and creative subjects were shunted aside as peripheral frills. In addition, the demand for teachers came to be so great that the shortages became politically dangerous to those in power. Attempts were made to recruit a sufficient number of candidates for the teaching profession by providing all sorts of "degrading" incentives, and by minimizing the importance of professional training. Short, inferior, crash programs were introduced in a number of provinces. Only now are Canadian politicians learning that this method of recruiting teachers will not secure greater numbers; it simply secures inferior quality. The proper method of securing more teachers is to raise standards, prolong the teacher training period, and make teaching an attractive profession, with a prestige equal to that of the other competing professions. In this way one improves not only the quantity, but also the quality. Luckily, in British Columbia we have succeeded in proving this point, and have made more significant progress toward the improvement of the educational system than has the rest of Canada.

Young people in Canada are less fearful of communism than those in the United States. They have noticed the emphasis the Russians are putting on education. They also see that Russians do not neglect cultural and creative subjects, even though they do put considerable stress on academic disciplines and science. In Canada, there is now a great wave of interest in making secondary education much more interesting, more attractive, and worthwhile for young people. There is a marked move toward the acceptance of music, fine arts, and theatre, home economics, and industrial education in the customary program for *all* students. Furthermore, even the academic subjects are becoming more practical and useful. Far more outdoor study is being provided in social studies where investigation and experiment with original documents and raw data are characteristic. Student-initiated experiments in all the sciences are now being promoted. Speech, theatre, and English are being combined. A root-and-branch reform of English grammar is taking place. Schools are becoming places where active inquiry and discovery are regularly undertaken in practical laboratory situations. Curricula are more closely related to activities in the outside world.

Young people see education as a process rather than as a product. Thinking skills are more important than the mere accumulation of information. Emphasis is being placed on the interest and value of study as an end in itself. The importance of encouraging enthusiasm, curiosity, and inquiry by providing a variety of opportunities for a great diversity of pupils is paramount. Schools are also assuming the important task of determining purposes and worthwhile continuing aims for young people. There is a feeling that young men and women are seeking new purposes and aims in life, and that schools should be places where young people discover an enduring life interest or hobby, or purpose or goal.

The gross hypocrisy, double talk, pretense, and sham of our adult society is being confronted by tremendous criticism. Young people insist on debating controversial issues. In the next twenty years there will be a return to simple honesty and integrity in an attempt to make the ethics taught in school and the moral behavior of human beings in our society at least similar, if not identical.

The effect of all the technical gains (such as programmed learning, television, and film) will be to upgrade the quality of educational activity. These devices will in no way reduce the need for teachers, nor do away with the personal interchange of ideas between the adult and the younger person. In fact, it seems quite clear the future will be a period when there will be far more and better teachers. Teachers, in turn, will demand more technical assistance and material aids.

If there is to be an improvement in the quality of education and the encouragement of young people to adopt a new set of values with much firmer purposes and objectives in their lives, there must be a reduction in the size of classes; there must be more opportunities for discussion and for debate; there must be more time allotted teachers for lesson preparation and more time for them to make thoughtful comments on the kinds of activities in which young people engage.

The next few years will see an advance, therefore, to an improved and revised form of progressive education, or to what many of us like to call "creative education." Obviously, far more money is going to be needed if we are to keep abreast of educational developments. The democratic ideals of Canada, as well as those of the United States, must be kept alive through renewed emphasis on upgrading the all-round education of our youth in the cultural and practical, as well as in the academic areas.

Education South of the Border

Herbert B. Wilson

In the immense region of the world lying south of the Rio Grande border, the land surface includes a tremendous amount of natural resources and a many-faceted population about equal in number to the populations of the United States and Canada combined. One finds it very easy to refer to the "Spanish-speaking" world, but there is Brazil with its Portuguese background, Haiti with its French influence, and several other nations and colonies reflecting other kinds of cultures and influences.

There is, however, a commonality among the peoples of the nations south of our border. In general, they are a mixed racial and ethnic group, with a high residual of native influence in their cultures, their languages, and their levels of aspiration. This is a young part of the world in many ways—in population for example, about 40 percent of the people south of the border are under fifteen years of age.

The nations of Latin America have many characteristics in common. There is what Oscar Lewis might refer to as a generalized "culture of poverty," because such conditions exist in all of the countries.[1] And, there are the kinds of conditions Lewis specifically refers to in his book, *La Vida*.[2] There is a dependence on a

---

[1] Oscar Lewis, *Five Families* (New York: Basic Books, 1959).
[2] Oscar Lewis, *La Vida* (New York: Random House, 1966).

cash economy, an overabundance of the labor force, low incomes, illiteracy, poor health conditions, little opportunity for upward mobility, and undereducation or lack of education entirely.

Only about half of the children of primary age in Latin America are attending school, and 78 percent of them drop out before completing a secondary education. Possibly half of the teachers have a degree, and in all Latin America (with a total population of 210 million in 1966), only 600,000 adolescents are enrolled in higher education. At the university level, only 2 percent of this number are matriculating students. During the 1964 World Education Assembly in Mexico City, a basic educational program was developed for Latin America. The following objectives were outlined:

1. Education should be national, with emphasis on history and democratic traditions.
2. Education should be democratic, with equality of opportunity.
3. Education should be popular, and serve the masses.
4. Education should be scientifically based.
5. Education should be productive, linking itself to manual labor and the machine age.[3]

In this general setting then, with attention focused specifically on Mexico, we must recognize that the subject of education in Mexico is a most complex one. A number of students from the University of Arizona in Tucson, visiting public schools in Nogales, Sonora (about an hour's drive from their campus), have been heard to observe on their return, "Well, this isn't the real Mexico–this is a border town and doesn't reflect the kind of thing that exists in the Republic." But the schools in Nogales, Sonora, do reflect conditions of education throughout Mexico, and the best answer to the students' observation would be, "What flag do the youngsters salute? Who is their president? What is their official language? What are their opportunities? What methods do they use–what kind of examination system? What kind of texts? What is the expectant level of participation, and what is the function of the teacher?" These are the important questions to ask!

---

[3]*The Times (London) Educational Supplement* (No. 2581), Nov. 6, 1964, p. 805.

Jules Henry, in his article "A Cross-Cultural Analysis of Education," has provided some very helpful questions in a similar vein which would assist in analyzing any educational system. He asks, "On what does the educational process focus? How is this information communicated? What methods are used? Who educates? How do the educators participate? Who is being educated? What limits the quantity and the quality of education? And what is the relationship between the intent and the outcome of education? What are the chief bases and sources for making educational decisions?"[4] With such questions, one could go into a classroom in any public school in Mexico and attempt to analyze the system and the institutional practices that reflect the national emphases on education.

Mexico is very rich in undeveloped natural resources. It is a nation with approximately the population of France, a capitol city larger than Paris, and with a cultural history and tradition that could be examined today and lead the investigator into some exciting research. Mexico has not rejected its historical tradition nor its culture, pockets of which still remain almost unchanged in attitude, language commitment, and learning from the days of the Conquistadores.

Mexico has been slow to change, but there are reasons for its delayed entry into the technological age. For example, most of the history of public education in Mexico has occurred during the past fifty years. The great excitement of the postrevolutionary period which initiated the establishment of the modern Mexican educational system began in the 1920s, but data is difficult to obtain, either from English or Spanish sources. It is as if the outside world has not been overly concerned with the development of education in Mexico, after the initial thrust of interest that occurred in the 1930s and early 1940s. While children in the Southwestern United States were growing up, going to structured school systems that were highly developed and articulated, a few miles away a nation was beginning to struggle for the development that would bring about dramatic changes in the lives and history of its people.

---

[4]Jules Henry, "A Cross-Cultural Analysis of Education," *Current Anthropology*, Vol. 1, No. 4 (July 1960), 267-305.

Five Major Periods of Mexican Educational Development

The first of five major periods of Mexican education may be classified as *Pre-Columbian*.[5] Before the fall of the Aztec empire to Cortés, education was focused mainly on religious and warlike ideals, and on the transmission of ancient culture to maintain social classes and the social conditions as well as religious faith. Public education did not begin until the age of fourteen. The Aztecs had religious and military schools, and the children who were selected for education were taught arithmetic, astronomy, botany, zoology, and to decipher hieroglyphics. Military science was always taught in a very practical way. Intellectual studies were rudimentary and related to religion. Sports, games, and music were part of the total program. The Mayans also included astronomy and mathematics, as well as writing, painting, and sculpture. Education was primarily a male pursuit, except for the girls who dedicated their lives to religion and who were sent to special schools.

The second period could be classified as the *Colonial* period. During this time, the Church, assisted by the royal crown of Spain, provided the nucleus of western educational development initiated in the New World. Thus, in a sense, an attempt was made to educate the Indians as the Church accepted the responsibility for educating both the Indian masses and the privileged Europeans. The Europeans brought to the New World the kind of institutions with which they were familiar in Spain. Along with teaching a new language and a new religion, missionaries gave the Indians the opportunity to learn many arts and crafts popular on the Continent. These included carpentry, blacksmithing, and shoemaking. It was at the beginning of this period that a need arose for the development of universities in the New World. The first university was developed in Peru, the second, in Mexico City. The focus was on educating the elite, with great emphasis on acquiring an education for scholastic purposes.

---

[5] Marjorie C. Johnston, *Education in Mexico* (Washington D.C.: U.S. Department of Health, Education, and Welfare, 1956).
Francisco Larroyo, *Historia Comparada de la Educación en México* (México, D.F.: Editorial Porrua, S.A., 1947).
Ramón Eduardo Ruiz, *Mexico, The Challenge of Poverty and Illiteracy* (San Marino, California: The Huntington Library, 1963).

The third phase could be classified as education during the *Independence* period. It was through this period following the 1820s that a growing desire for an organized, free public education program, open to all social classes, became apparent. A new and practical teacher-education program was required as well as the establishment of schools to accommodate the growing concerns of a developing nation. Progress was very slow, however, and mass education was not achieved.

The fourth period could be considered the *Reform Movement*. It was through the efforts of Benito Juárez that education underwent a theoretical change. Education was declared both free and compulsory. The teaching of religion was to be excluded completely from the public schools. Secondary schools were organized—a secondary school for girls was founded, and the national preparatory school. Much of the development was observed only in aspiration and not in actual practice. Then, during the 35-year regime of Porfirio Díaz (the period known as Porfirism), additional reforms were introduced in the educational program. Despite all the efforts made by the government concerning education, however, the number of illiterates at the end of the nineteenth century was overwhelming. It was during the 1910 Revolution that education really became a focus of national interest. Somehow, the people believed they were fighting a revolution for land and for education, as indicated by Lloyd H. Hughes in *The Mexican Cultural Mission Programme*.[6] One of the major battle cries of the Revolution was "Educar es redimir" ("To educate is to redeem").

The period of *Modern Mexican Education*, the fifth stage of the educational evolution, began with the *Constitution of 1917*. Article III of this dramatic document triggered the explosive development of modern education in Mexico. The path was uneven to be sure, but the school system was secularized with the conviction that education "is the monopoly of all the people of the state, and not of one group, whether that group be of the Church or professional educators." But Article III did not provide for a ministry of education. José Vasconcelos, now acclaimed as

[6]Lloyd H. Hughes, *The Mexican Cultural Mission Programme* (Paris: UNESCO, 1950).

the "father of modern Mexican education," designed a blueprint for a federal Ministry of Education which permitted federal officials to establish primary schools throughout the Republic.[7] Vasconcelos became the first Secretary of Public Education in 1921. He used an old convent on Calle Argentina as his headquarters. The "Casa on Calle Argentina," as it became known, was the focal point of many educational innovations and reforms.

To effect the dream of the Revolution and accommodate all factions within the power groups of the Republic were not easy tasks. The political struggle was strongly philosophical in origin. On the continuum of decision, the new intellectuals of the Mexican Revolution were faced with many major problems. The notion of education as redemption suggested that social reform depended upon the quality and the philosophic commitment of the educational development. On one hand were the conservatives, as represented predominantly by the Church, and on the other hand were the liberals, who had taken the philosophy of John Dewey and modified its application to the Mexican problems. Ruiz pointed out that Dewey's *School and Society* "had a wide reading public among teachers who came to believe that the solution to Mexico's problems lay in his theory. . . . Dewey was gospel among Mexican teachers."[8]

There were other related decisions regarding the focus of education. One segment of the population, represented by Vasconcelos, was concerned with the notion of Europeanizing the Mexican people. This was the *indigenistas* point of view. They considered the function of the school as that of making the modern world intelligible to the Indians and linking the primitive with the modern. On the other hand, Gamio and some others were committed to the *indianismo* concept, or the notion that schools should restore pre-Columbian culture to the Indians. It was a sentimental and romantic point of view, based on pride of race, the awakening of folk language, and a blend of pagan worship and Catholicism. What emerged was what Ruiz classifies as the Mexicanization, or the blending of all strains of Mexican society

---

[7]Ramón Eduardo Ruiz, *Mexico, The Challenge of Poverty and Illiteracy* (San Marino, California: The Huntington Library, 1963).
[8]*Ibid.*

enriched by the contributions of both points of view. Gamio moved to this middle-of-the-road position, insisting that the combination of both was best; the pre-Hispanic and colonial legacy combined with the best elements of the western culture that might be adaptable to the nature of the individual's particular needs and aspirations.

In this struggle of cultural change, the institutions that had the most to lose fought vigorously to maintain the *status quo*. Twice during the first fifteen years of the newly developing educational system (which was growing in its socialistic tendency), the emerging philosophy was violently attacked. The Cristeros, a fanatical but not official movement of Church members, fought the anticlerical mood of the liberal movement in education. Ruiz tells us that "Shouting 'Long live Christ, the King,' peasants battled peasants, schools were burned, and teachers (and priests) were beaten and even murdered."[9] The struggle of separating church and state in education has been a persistent and continuing one in Mexico. The revision of Article III promoted even greater conflicts and outrages.

By the time the National Revolutionary Party Convention was held in October, 1933, Article III was amended to form the basis of the Mexican Socialistic Schools. Some of the aims and limits of education provided in this revision were:

1. The education imparted by the State shall be a socialistic one and, in addition to excluding all religious doctrine, shall combat fanaticism and prejudices by organizing its instruction and activities in a way that shall permit the creation in youth of an exact and rational concept of the Universe and of social life.
2. Only the State–Federation, States, Municipalities–shall impart primary, secondary, and normal education. Authorization may be conceded to individuals who desire to impart education in any of the aforementioned three levels in conformity, in every case, with the following norms:
   a. The teachings and activities of private plants must adjust themselves without exception to that indicated in the initial paragraph of this article, and shall be in charge of persons who, in the opinion of the State, shall have sufficient professional preparation and a morality and ideology that is suitable to and in keeping with this precept. In view of this, religious corporations, ministers of cults, the organizations which preferably or exclusively carry on educational activities,

[9] *Ibid.*

and the associations or societies bound directly or indirectly to the propaganda of a religious creed, shall in no way intervene in primary, secondary, or normal schools, nor shall they be permitted to assist these financially.

b. The formation of plans, programmes, and methods of teaching shall in every case rest in the State.

c. Private plants shall not be permitted to function without first, and in each case, having obtained the express authorization of the public power.

d. The State may at any time revoke the authorization granted. . . . The same norms shall govern education of whatever type or grade. . . . Primary education shall be obligatory, and the State shall impart it gratuitously.

3. The State may, at its discretion and at any time, withdraw recognition of official validity to the studies made in private plants. . . .[10]

The Mexican educational system was considered an instrument to bring about social and cultural revolution. The socialistic school was designed to be proletarian, popular, and nationalistic. Its chief interest was in the unification and nationalization of the masses for their benefit and interest.[11] It was also designed to be a rationalistic school, in order to inculcate beliefs that would stand the test of intellectual and rational examination. On this basis, the development of the educational program began to accelerate throughout the Republic.

The Secretary of Public Education, reinforced by the strong stand taken by the federal government, removed all secondary education from private control. In 1934, under the regime of Cardenas, the socialistic schools became more and more influential. By 1945, however, there was a modification to the socialistic nature of the schools when it was recognized that other institutions could contribute to the developing educational pattern in Mexico. Strong feelings on both sides of the religious conflict involved in the development of public education were apparent

---

[10]Marjorie C. Johnston, *Education in Mexico* (Washington, D.C.: U.S. Department of Health, Education, & Welfare, 1956).
Francisco Larroyo, *Historia Comparada de la Educación en Mexico* (México, D.F.: Editorial Porrua, S.A., 1947).
George I. Sanchez, *Mexico, A Revolution by Education* (New York: The Viking Press, 1936).

[11]George C. Booth, *Mexico's School-Made Society* (Stanford, California: Stanford University Press, 1941).

throughout the Republic. Now there is a mood of conciliation in the idea that the public schools and the Church can find ways of working together. Even today, however, the Church has not recognized the fact that the public schools in Mexico are there to stay. Parochial schools are being used to supplant public schools, rather than to fill the void. Ruiz suggests that if the public schools in Mexico are to survive, the Mexican government needs to control the Church's educational development more than it has in recent years.[12]

The Structure of Public Education

The structure of public education in Mexico reflects the European tradition, with special emphasis on the French system. The focus on "intellectualism" is apparent. Mexican education is highly centralized within the framework of federal regulations. While schools exist on the municipal, state, and federal levels, all technical direction is under federal control. This includes statements of objectives, programs of study, methods of instruction, and examinations. The Secretary of Public Education is the highest authority for education; he is appointed by the president and serves on his cabinet. Several other secretariats, however, have jurisdiction over special types of education. Higher schools of agriculture come under the Secretary of Agriculture, military schools under the direction of the Secretary of National Defense, and preschool education (except *jardín de niños*) is under the Secretary of Health and Welfare. The National Autonomous University of Mexico controls the preparatory schools, the national schools of music and fine arts, and the approved institutions of higher education (except technical education) in the states.

Education in each state, except for federal schools, is the responsibility of the Director General of Education, who is appointed by the governor of the state. The Director General, in turn, appoints a Director of Inspection and a Director of Finance, who are professionally trained. While municipalities establish and maintain the schools, the state authorities appoint and supervise

---

[12] Ramón Eduardo Ruiz, *Mexico, The Challenge of Poverty and Illiteracy* (San Marino, California: The Huntington Library, 1963).

the teachers. Taxes in support of education vary in each state. To alleviate deficiences in local and state systems, since 1922 the federal government has been developing a federally supported school system. The federal Secretary of Public Education maintains a Director of Federal Education in each state capitol to control all federal schools within the state and to coordinate federal activities with local and state authorities.

A good example of different kinds of schools in the various parts of Mexico can be found in Nogales, Sonora. Although a few teachers are paid out of municipal funds, there are no municipal schools in Nogales. There are nine state elementary schools, one federal elementary school, and two private or church-oriented elementary schools, plus a number of *jardines de niños*, both public and private. The secondary school is a federal school; the technical or vocational school is federal- and state-supported. The preparatory school is governed by the National University in Mexico City. The rural schools around Nogales are predominantly federal schools, except for a few supported by the state.

The academic ability and professional or vocational interests of the student tend to stratify the direction and level of education. There are many curriculum tracks, but the three major ones are: a university education, a normal school education, and a technical and professional education.

In general, the public school system provides for six years of primary education, beginning at age six. Many areas provide a kindergarten program, and in a few urban areas there are even some "infant schools" before the kindergarten level. The six years of primary school, from ages six to fourteen inclusive, are, by law, free, secular, and compulsory. As noted previously, however, in practice, less than half of the youngsters of school age in Mexico are attending school.

There is a three-year secondary school which includes seventh, eighth, and ninth grades. Those going on to higher education in the university system leave the secondary school and attend the two-year preparatory school, thus obtaining a five-year secondary education. After preparatory school, the students going into some professions and into higher studies attend the university from three to seven years.

To become a teacher in the elementary school system, one would go from the three-year secondary school to the normal school where, generally, there would be three years of instruction before being granted a teaching certificate.[13] Quite often, however, students are in the field teaching before they complete their three years of normal school, and are teaching on what might be considered "provisional certificates" here. They return to school during vacations to complete their requirements. It is possible that after three years of normal school, a student can enter and go on to the higher normal school, which would carry him through another four years of education and give him the highest degree he can earn in elementary teaching. Those who intend to teach at the secondary level generally must go through the secondary school, the preparatory school, and the university system. There is yet another track following primary school, which is a preprofessional secondary program of three years, followed by vocational school for two years, and then a technical school at various professional levels. The engineers, pharmacists, biologists, and other similar professions, move on this track rather than through the university system.

The program of study in the majority of elementary and secondary schools is fairly academic with national uniformity.[14] The scope and sequence tends to be controlled by federal regulations, federally supplied texts and workbooks, federal supervision and inspection, and the centralized examination program. Subjects taught each year include language, arithmetic and geometry, science, geography, history, civics, drawing, music and singing, manual arts for boys, home economics for girls, and physical education. The examinations, prepared for each grade and subject by the Instituto Nacional de Pedagogía, are sent to zone inspectors for distribution to the teachers. The teachers receive precise directions for giving the tests, including time limits, a key for scoring, and a scale for grading.

---

[13]Union Pan-Americana. Departamento de Asuntos Educativos. *La Formación del Profesorado de las Escuelas Normales Latinas Americanas* (Washington, D.C., 1964).

[14]C. Alberto Castro Flores, *Nuevo Programa de Educación, Soxto Ecado* (México, D.F.: Editorial Avante, 1966).

At the present time, there are two Educational Zones in Mexico. Zone A cuts across the Republic from east to west at the State of Jalisco, where Guadalajara is located, and extends south. The long vacation for Zone A starts in December and ends in February. Zone B, encompassing all the states north of this line, has the long vacation from the end of June to the end of August. However, this practice is expected to change within the next year or two, so that all the schools in Mexico will operate on the same calendar.

Problems in Education in Mexico

There have been a number of attempts to bring about a mass educational change in Mexico since the 1920s. Each of these has been a fairly noble experiment—some of them being continued are having adequate results. The major problem confronting the nation since the 1920 Revolution has been the development of a literate population. Illiteracy rates have been extremely high; some estimates have been as high as 85 percent.[15] Of course, the classification of illiteracy varies from nation to nation. During the term of one social action program in Mexico, a person was considered literate who could read and write his own name. In the United States, a person is not considered functionally literate until he has completed the fourth grade.

In Mexico, a number of programs have been developed which operate outside the structure of public education previously indicated. One of the most important of these is the "Cultural Mission Program."[16] Originally, the Missions were designed to educate rural teachers for the recognized school system throughout the Republic. After a period of growth and then decline, the Cultural Missions were reestablished as community development centers. There is also an attempt to improve health, sanitation, and hygienic conditions through the Bien Estar Rural Program in rural parts of Mexico. And, early in the development of anti-illiteracy programs, the patranato system was established. In this program,

---

[15]Ruth I. Anderson, "Education in Mexico," *Business Education Forum,* Vol. 12, No. 6 (March 1958).

[16]*Ibid.*

each literate person was charged with the responsibility to teach one illiterate, a kind of "each-one-teach-one" program. Most of the anti-illiteracy programs focus on teaching Spanish as a *lingua franca*, although there was an attempt to teach literacy in the native language, somewhat following the mood of the *Indianistas*. This program became known as the *alfabetizadores*. There were also attempts to establish indigenous schools in Mexico City. It was soon discovered, however, that when rural people were taken to urban centers for instruction, it was difficult to get them to return to the rural environment.

Following World War II, UNESCO established its Fundamental Education Center for Latin America in the city of Patzcuaro, Mexico. This school was designed as one of the few international fundamental education centers sponsored by that organization. Delegations from all the republics in Latin America worked at the school as students, planning to return to their own countries to carry on the work of fundamental education following their graduation from the 18-month training program. Fundamental education very closely resembles the kind of program established by the Mexican Cultural Missions. Emphasis is placed on the development of literacy, on child care and home economics, on wise use of leisure time through healthy recreation, on agricultural assistance and economic development, and on community sanitation and hygiene.

There are many factors in Mexico which tend to retard and inhibit educational development. One of the major factors may be the conception of *la raza*, "affiliation of the race."[17] This ethnic affiliation, or "mystique," has tended to restrict the upward mobility of large groups of people. And, coupled with this idea is the image of the male and female in the Mexican culture. The concept of *macho* or *machismo*, the dominance of the male for control and superiority, has tended to be anti-intellectual until the recent development of the growing middle class in Mexico. It also has been discovered that no matter how enthusiastic and devoted

---

[17]Octavio Paz, *The Labyrinth of Solótude*, trans. by Lysander Kemp (New York: Grove Press, 1961).

anti-illiteracy workers might be, there are always more illiterates at the end of a program than when the program begins.[18] The vastly increasing birth rate has outstripped the gain made by the organized program to develop literacy throughout Mexico. Illiteracy now exists in about 40 percent of the population. There is, of course, a lack of materials, well-prepared teachers, buildings, and educational resources in every area of the Republic. The language problem is there—with the diversification of language patterns, the development of the *lingua franca*, or Spanish, has not gone ahead as originally planned.

One of the most difficult tasks is to get teachers into the rural areas following their teacher preparation program. Teachers now completing normal school (which generally turns out only elementary teachers) must now obligate the first two years of their professional career to working in the rural communities.

There is increasing unrest in all the student bodies of the universities in Mexico. For a number of weeks in 1965, the National University in Mexico City was under siege, and finally the rector was forced to resign from his post. This type of political involvement was noted most recently at the University of Sonora, an institution established in 1940. The students became involved in the selection of a governor for the state, and the uprising became so intense that an exchange program with students from the University of Arizona had to be cancelled.

In his 1966 State of the Union message to the Mexican people, President Ordaz reported the progress being made in all fields of social endeavor within the nation. He devoted a great deal of attention to the developing education program. He announced that 7,400,000 children were attending school throughout the Republic at that time, that 36 million textbooks had been given to youngsters in all the schools, and that federally printed and distributed texts ranged through all subjects in the primary schools in Mexico.[19] In contrast to only about 12 percent throughout Latin America, about 25 percent of the public funds in Mexico go to the educational enterprise.[20]

---

[18]Ramón Eduardo Ruiz, *Mexico, The Challenge of Poverty and Illiteracy* (San Marino, California: The Huntington Library, 1963).

[19]*El Heraldo de México* (México, D.F.), Sept. 2, 1966.
Novedades Diario De La Tarde, Sept. 1, 1966.

[20]*The Times (London) Educational Supplement* (No. 2581), Nov. 6, 1964, p. 805.

The leaders in Mexico recognize the tremendous need for future development in the nation, that labor needs are shifting from an agricultural economy to a technological one, and that the population must achieve a certain degree of educational literacy to function fully in this half of the twentieth century.

Educationally, however, Mexico has a long way to go. Thousands of prefabricated school buildings are being built every year in rural areas, with attractive audio-visual aids laminated into the plastic windows. More and more now, the French tradition of intellectual development is being supplanted by a pragmatic, more vocationally oriented program that involves the actual use of knowledge rather than its acquisition alone.

Education in the United States, too, is serving more as a model for Mexican educational development. While examinations are still centrally organized and administered, rote memory is now being modified to more problem solving and practical application of subject matter. These changes can be seen throughout the school system where, at the present time, greater emphasis is given to the development of *all* Mexicans in order that they may function more adequately in the twentieth century world.

The Mexican nation has yet to take its destined position of leadership in the family of nations. The time will come, however, when Mexico—with its growing desire and its energy for educational development—will not only maintain its leadership in Latin America, but will become a leader on the international scene. A nation with such resources and a developing literate population has only the need for improved educational opportunity to bring it to the point of making a maximum contribution to the world order.

Education in the Land of the Yeti

Hugh B. Wood

The Abominable Snowman, or Yeti, as he is known in the Himalayas, has become symbolic of the mysticism, the romance, and the mountainous terrain that characterize Nepal, a country that until a decade ago was little known to the outside world. In the brief span of a decade, however, Nepal has been visited by more than fifty thousand tourists from the Western Hemisphere, and has joined the world community of nations. At the present time, Nepal has embarked upon the difficult and often stormy sea of economic development. Certainly, Nepal wants to take her place among the significant nations of the world.

Before discussing education in Nepal, one should consider pertinent background factors. Sitting astride the great Himalayan Range, Nepal to the visitor is remote, beautiful, unusual, simple, primitive, and a photographer's paradise. To the philosophically inclined, Nepal is Shangri-La. There is scarcely another place in the world where one can find more peaceful and joyous satisfaction with life than in some of the remote mountain villages of this country. Economically, Nepal is among the least developed countries of the world. There is a high illiteracy rate, and it is said that in 1950 this proportion of the population reached 99 percent. A high percentage of the labor force is engaged in agriculture. In 1950, only three small factories existed; eight had been established by 1961. A most primitive transportation system exists; currently there are only 400 miles of jeepable and graveled roads. There is one commercial bank, a few facilities for systematically collecting economic and demographic statistics, and individual income has been estimated to be only $12.00 in cash or $40.00 in "kind" per year.

Historically, Nepal was an aggregation of loosely related, often warring principalities. During the latter part of the eighteenth century (1743-1816), Prithwi Narayan Shah and his successors united the area known today as Nepal. From 1846 to 1950, the country was ruled by a family of dictators, and was rigidly closed to all foreigners. In 1951, the royal family of Prithwi Narayan Shah resumed control, solicited foreign aid, and set the stage for the long struggle of economic development and independence.

Each of these factors, and many others, play an important role in the development of education in Nepal. They contribute to the uniqueness of some characteristics of the educational development.

There are three conditions that have affected the basic procedures in designing an educational program for Nepal. First, unlike many developing countries, Nepal did not have existing educational facilities when missions from the United States and elsewhere arrived to help plan the educational program. Under the Rana dictatorship, to give or receive learning was a capital offense. Missionaries had been excluded from the country, and Nepal rigorously avoided any type of colonial status. Thus, one could not find an educational structure similar to those observed in most developing countries today.

A largely unsuccessful attempt was made in 1948 to introduce "basic education" from India. A few Sanskrit schools were also established. Essentially, however, a vacuum existed insofar as education was concerned and, consequently, the planners had a relative amount of freedom in developing an educational system for Nepal.

Second, there was scarcely a national plan, or identified national goal, to serve as a framework for the design and development of a national educational system. Because of the change from a dictatorship to a democratic monarchy, and the abruptness with which leadership had shifted to the royal family, a national educational system had not developed. Further, the lack of good communication and dissemination systems, and the very lack of education among the people of the country, remained inhibiting factors to a national system of education. Indeed, by 1950 Nepal had not reached the first step of economic development or promulgated a national economic plan.

In his early pronouncements as national leader, King Tribhuvan stated that he desired a democratic form of government, education for his people, and relief from sickness and poverty. Of course, he indicated his desire for general economic improvement and actively solicited foreign aid. But, beyond this, there was little direction or guidance for planning an educational system. Even the several political parties were much more concerned with political than with social or economic goals.

Third, the lack of schools, the government dictatorship, and the absence of a colonial power all contributed to dearth of human leadership in both government and education. Within the total population of nearly nine million people, in 1950 there were about three hundred who had completed their college work, one thousand who had finished secondary school programs, and perhaps only one hundred thousand who might be considered literate. Less than five hundred persons had had any experience in government and most of these only at the clerical level; perhaps fifty persons had held top-echelon positions within the government. In 1954, there was an attempt to recruit persons to be trained in the United States to serve as a College of Education staff in Nepal, but only eleven could be found who held the baccalaureate degree and were interested in improving education. Indeed, only one person in the entire country held the Master of Education degree.

Because of these conditions, it seemed imperative that any mission from the United States should begin by establishing a National Education Planning Commission of outstanding lay and education leaders in Nepal. The U.S. Commission, therefore, undertook (a) the survey of existing educational services, facilities, and resources; (b) the consideration of present and projected educational needs at all levels; (c) a tentative statement of national goals and aspirations as a philosophical base on which to develop an educational system; and (d) the design of a complete educational system and program for Nepal. After a year of deliberations, and more than one hundred meetings, the

Commission published a report that subsequently received the King's "seal," and has been used for thirteen years as the guide for detailed educational planning and development in that country.[1]

The major educational goals set by the Commission included (a) universal, free, compulsory primary education by 1985; (b) free multipurpose (vocational) secondary education available on a ratio of one school for every ten thousand people by 1975; (c) coordinated higher education under a national residential university by 1965; and (d) adult education for all who desired it by 1965. Supporting services were also to be provided and would include teacher training; textbook preparation, publication, and distribution; special technical training as needed; organization of appropriate administration; supervision and research facility planning; and sources for the financing of education.

These goals proved to be too ambitious for achievement within the dates set, but in 1962 a UNESCO team visiting Nepal found that considerable progress had been made. Sixteen percent of the elementary-age children were in school, a number of multipurpose high schools had been established, a national university had been chartered, and fifty thousand adults had enrolled in literacy classes. Teacher-training programs had been firmly established and a Bureau of Publications was functioning. Also, twenty-four technical training institutions had been established. The coordination of higher education, however, had not been achieved. Administration and supervision were improving, and financing was forthcoming but somewhat limited. Of course, all this progress had been matched with problems that needed to be resolved.[2]

Establishing an Educational System

Let us now turn to some of the ways, often unique, in which some of the problems were met in Nepal. First, the lack of any major foreign school system, but some experience at the local level

---

[1]Rudra Raj Pandey, Kaisher Bahadur, K. C., and Hugh B. Wood, *Education in Nepal: Report of the National Education Planning Commission.* Katmandu: Bureau of Publishing, College of Education, 1956. (U.S. Distribution: American Nepal Education Foundation, Box 5123, Eugene. Oregon.)

[2]Hugh B. Wood, and Bruno Knall, *Educational Planning in Nepal and Its Economic Implications* (Paris: UNESCO, 1962). Also: *Educational Statistics for Nepal.* Eugene, Oregon: American Nepal Education Foundation, 1962.

with five different types of schools (Compas, English, Sanskrit, Vernacular, and Basic) provided an opportunity to examine the advantages and limitations of various forms of education without external pressure and to design a curriculum suited to the needs of the Nepalese people. At the primary level, the curriculum developed around three primary areas: "Feeding Ourselves," "Clothing Ourselves," and "Housing Ourselves," and was aimed at providing functional literacy. The secondary school curriculum was to be multipurpose and oriented to occupational training.

Second, because of the lack of a national plan and a pool of trained human resources, the National Educational Planning Commission held meetings whereby national economic and educational orientation for all fifty-six members was provided. The result was the development of a strong cadre of well-informed leaders who were subsequently placed in high positions of national importance. This technique proved to be good insurance many times during past years and (both politically and financially) educational development in Nepal has progressed through the emergence of this strong leadership group.

Third, to meet the immediate demand for trained educational personnel, a somewhat elaborate system of teacher education was organized. The training of a faculty for a College of Education was initiated. During the first year, the training consisted of a daily two-hour seminar, followed by the group's serving as a "Normal School" staff for the remainder of the day. This procedure served the dual purpose of producing some primary school teachers with whom schools might start immediately and provided on-the-job experience for the future teachers' college staff. During the second year, the group was afforded an opportunity to study at the University of Oregon where, together with extensive consultant services and observations in various teacher-training institutions, details of the Nepalese College of Education were planned. Simultaneously, each member of the future college staff studied his preassigned specialty and obtained a master's degree. Within a month after returning to Katmandu, the College of Education was training the Normal School staff members who, in turn, were training primary school teachers within the year. Within another year, the primary schools were opened in Nepal. At the present time, the College of Education also trains school administrators and secondary school teachers.

Fourth, there were several problems relating to the training of primary school teachers. Both teacher candidates and the various local communities disliked mobility. They preferred training offered close to their homes and their ultimate assignments. Lack of transportation made training at a centralized location quite impractical. And yet, few local or hinterland areas could utilize the output from a Normal School, even as small a group as thirty trainees per year. This was further complicated by the simultaneous need for teachers in every part of the country.

To meet these problems a central, but unique, scheme was determined. A dozen mobile Normal School teams rotated annually among the thirty-two regional district headquarters. In this way, they could reach each area every third year or so. Each team of six included specialists in psychology and principles of learning, communication skills, agriculture and science, home crafts and art, the social sciences, and health and physical education. Each team carried its own library and textbooks. Facilities were rented or constructed of bamboo and thatch. These facilities were often converted into a model primary school during the final two months of training. When the teacher-education program had been completed, the facilities were donated to the village. During the first ten days after arrival at the site, the team would disperse to the neighboring villages to recruit candidates. There was an attempt to enlist from thirty to seventy-five trainees for each team. Following recruitment, there was an eight-month training period and finally a two- or three-week "field" experience during which the staff assisted the new teachers in opening schools in their own villages. The staff would then return to Katmandu for a six-week refresher workshop, thirty days of rest, and then reassignment.[3]

It should be pointed out that the primary schools were usually opened with a first grade of about thirty pupils. Another teacher was added the second year, and another first grade group as the original group advanced to the second grade. When five grades were operating, a second section of the first grade was opened, and

---

[3]Hugh B. Wood, "Mobile Normal Schools in Nepal," *Comparative Education*, 1:119-24, (March 1965); and *Manual for Training Teachers.* Katmandu: Bureau of Publishing, College of Education, 1956.

so on. Nepal has adopted the 5-5 pattern of education. With the availability of newly trained teachers generally limited to every third year, it was expected that about two-thirds of the teachers would be untrained. However, after a short period of time about half of the teachers were untrained; this was attributed to a certain amount of mobility throughout the land. When the mobile team returned to the area, these untrained teachers were released either for a year's training or for "short courses" of two to four weeks offered by the team members.

Fifth, the country's educational plan called for an attack on literacy at both the child and adult level. The dual problems of a supply of teachers to accomplish these objectives and a choice of sites for both types of classes were met by asking primary school teachers to teach literacy classes, and by giving priority to villages willing to open a primary school and an adult literacy class at the same time. Furthermore, in choosing pupils to be admitted to the new classes, priority was given to children whose parents enrolled in literacy classes, and to parents whose children enrolled in primary classes. The mutual support and encouragement provided by this "family plan" has been very effective.

Continuing Problems in Nepal

One might comment briefly on several problems of a serious nature within Nepal that are also found in other developing countries. First, the secondary school-age population (11-15) is increasing more rapidly than the secondary school enrollment. Although secondary school facilities are being added continuously, the percentage of school-age children attending school at this level is decreasing and will continue to decrease for at least another ten years. The reasons for this decrease relate to a lack of funds, a concentration of funds and efforts on primary education, and the effect of reducing the infant mortality rate through preventive health measures. To correct this condition would require an alteration of one or more of these three causes, and, of course, one cannot see any substantial change in any of them in the immediate future.

Further, there exists in Nepal, as in many other countries —including America—a general dislike, if not disdain, for vocational education. This type of training implies manual labor, which the caste system—formally in Nepal, informally in America—relegates to low status. Education is held to be synonymous with professional, high government, and business occupations. It has been difficult to have the Nepalese accept the multipurpose, vocational concept of secondary education and to interest young people in being trained as vocational teachers. Nor are high school students counseled into vocational education. Advancement toward this goal continues to meet resistance in Nepal in spite of financial and/or other inducements.

There has also been an extremely unhealthy and uncontrolled proliferation of colleges in Nepal since 1950. There were only two colleges in existence at that time, but by 1954 there were fourteen, by 1961 thirty-three, and now there are probably more than fifty. This has resulted in an attempt to gain prestige quickly. The weaknesses of the government agencies and the University Commission designed to control the situation are noticeable and the politicians refuse to discourage "founders" of such institutions. The universal difficulty of imposing blocks and division in the educational ladder is also apparent. In 1961, a UNESCO survey team found that eighteen of the twenty-nine nonprofessional colleges had less than one hundred students enrolled. One had only six students and six faculty members. Nine had less than four hundred students.

College faculties are poorly trained. Libraries and laboratories are largely nonexistent and facilities extremely poor; at times these universities are located within an individual's home. The UNESCO team made strong recommendations to limit development to one university and nine or ten colleges, including six professional colleges. No observable action has yet been taken to cope with the problem, and indeed it is one of the pressing problems throughout the country of Nepal.

The same situation has developed in technical training. In 1961, there were twenty-four institutions training in five general fields. The UNESCO team recommended consolidation into five institutions, but each of the twenty-four has been a special project of some foreign-aid donor and thus it has been easier to ignore the problem than to cope with it.

In Nepal, as elsewhere, the traditional European-oriented examination system has resulted in a tremendous human wastage. The present secondary school, with its heavy academic emphasis, still requires a completion examination of the "Cambridge type." The colleges, largely British-oriented because of their affinity with Indian universities, require examinations after the second and fourth years. The attrition rate on all three of these examinations averages 60-65 percent. The successful baccalaureate candidate thus is automatically in the upper 5 percent of those who attended the secondary school and attempted the secondary school examination. Although the evils of this system are recognized, the practice is sometimes defended on the grounds that it helps to maintain standards in the absence of well-qualified teachers and adequate facilities and it controls enrollments in higher education.

There has been, and continues to be, an imbalance in the development of the various facets in Nepal's economic "plans." For example, by 1961, educational development had utilized 112 percent of the development funds allocated to it since 1954. Other governmental services had utilized from 22 percent to 76 percent of their allocated funds. This resulted in a suggestion by the Planning Council that funds for education be either cut drastically or entirely eliminated until the other sectors of the economy "caught up." This, of course, completely ignored the human and financial wastage, to say nothing of social deterioration that would result from such action. Haphazard "tooling up" and "untooling" or "stair-step" progress is uneconomical when applied to physical resources; it is disastrous when applied to human resources.[4]

Certainly, the educational program in Nepal is built on bedrock. Planning is evident. But education does suffer from inadequate financial and human resources, sometimes internal petty jealousies, and interference of vested-interest-dominated aid-donors. The usual problems that beset education in both developing and developed countries are noted throughout Nepal. Without question, however, education in Nepal has surpassed the "take-off" point of "no return," and will continue to expand and improve, even if sometimes it appears that progress is sporadic. Yes, formal education has finally come to the Land of the Yeti, and only the future can tell if these peoples who live on the roof of the world will be made happier through a knowledge of life and its potential.

---

[4]Hugh B. Wood, "Problems of Educational Planning in Nepal," *The Educational Forum*, 29:44-49, (Nov. 1964).

The New Education in Africa

Marsden B. Stokes

Africa is a land of seemingly limitless resources and possibilities for development. Huge areas await the time when man will subdue them and direct their use to his higher purposes—Ethiopia alone has the potential to produce enough food to feed the whole of Europe.

The problems of poverty, disease, inadequate transportation and communication facilities, and illiteracy (with its attendant ignorance and superstition) continue to retard the progress of the various African people of many races, colors, and creeds; this is a matter of grave concern to enlightened people everywhere. Vastly expanded programs of modern education are needed to unlock the shackles that impede the full development of the capabilities, both physical and intellectual, of the African people in the developing nations.

Let us see what some of the action is on the African educational scene as we consider "The New Education in Africa" and, more particularly, in Ethiopia.

Tribal and Community Influences

To understand the educational strivings of the African peoples today, it is necessary to be aware of the influences of the past. We should recognize that tribal influences, some of hundreds of years' standing, still are effective determinants of national policy in the

African nations. Recall the recent turmoil in Nigeria, a nation many of us believed to be as stable and well established as any of the newer countries on the continent. Only time will tell whether tribal loyalties will prove stronger in Nigeria and a number of other nations than the forces building toward a national life.

The situation in Uganda before the arrival of the missionaries was typical of tribal influences in education. As David Scanlon has pointed out, education there was carried out privately in the various tribal groups. He says,

> . . . Among the Nilotic people, it was customary for young people to attend meetings of the elders who heard discussions of disputes among the people of the community. In this way, it was felt the youth would learn the laws and customs of the people. Youths from the royal families of the Buganda Kingdom were trained as pages in the royal courts. By this method they became acquainted with the outstanding people of the country and brought into the operation of the kingdom.[1]

Even today, village elders still meet for discussion and decision making. As one travels through portions of East Africa, he can see these men gathered together in council under convenient but isolated shade trees, just outside the village. From their parents, from the elders, and from the community, the children and youth still learn many patterns of acceptable conduct in social, economic, political, and religious areas.

Religious and Colonial Influences

We cannot discuss many of the other background influences and early educational forms in Ethiopia. We should understand, however, that religious groups of ancient descent have played and continue to play prominent roles in educational matters. For example, for hundreds of years the Ethiopian Orthodox Church has preserved writings of the ancient Ge'ez language, a language as related to modern Amharic as Latin is to present-day Italian.

As in centuries past, the priests in the church schools continue to teach reading, writing, religion, some basics of ethics and morals

---

[1]David Scanlon, *Education In Uganda*, (U.S. Department of Health, Education and Welfare, Office of Education, Bulletin 1964), No. 32 (OE 14103). Washington, D.C.: Government Printing Office, 1964.

(as the priests see them), and a few other fundamentals of learning. These schools, often held in church compounds, perhaps under trees, are living testimony that the old education exists side by side with the new.

Remnants of colonialism may also be observed in present-day African educational systems. Teaching methods, curriculum content, instructional and administrative organization, and emphasis on examinations illustrate this point. Even the all too prevalent attitude that physical labor is somehow degrading may be traced, at least in part, to the examples set in years past by colonial overlords.[2]

The Old Education

The old education in Africa overemphasized content while giving little attention to the learner and his needs. It was too often characterized by a situation wherein the teacher dictated from his copy book (or wrote on a chalkboard if he had one) while the pupils recorded the same material word for word in their copy books for memorization and parrotlike repetition. It stressed preparation for examinations which called for the repetition of the information that had been memorized rather than a demonstration of insight, comprehensive understanding, and ability to apply what had been learned in meaningful situations. Education looked to the voice of authority even when empirical evidence was available and was prone to leave its students with neither the spark of initiative nor inquiring minds. It looked to the past rather than to the future. Unfortunately, too much of this type of education is still found in Africa. But enough of this—what of the new?

The New Education

As M. Sequaries, lecturer in Educational Psychology at Dakar, has said,

> Like every revolutionary movement, modern teaching methods set out to change this above-mentioned unprofitable system with a view to making

---

[2]Many Ethiopian students have long fingernails on their little fingers to indicate that they do not perform physical labor. I am reminded of a bright eighth grade graduate, desperately seeking financial help to stay in school, who said, "If I don't get more education, I'll either have to go to work or live by my wits!"

education more dramatic. The child became the central concern and an attempt was made to extend the concepts taught as he grew older and to . . . develop his intellectual abilities . . . rather than to induce automatic reactions while pre-mature emphasis on memory work was avoided.[3]

The new education in Africa is a more dynamic, on-going, outward-reaching, and positive institution. Defeatism and subjection are not its earmarks. It reflects almost an unrealistic "can do" image. It is championing the "Africa for the Africans" theme. To continue to put Africans in positions of authority and responsibility is one of its immediate and basic goals. It does not hesitate to borrow the good it can find in advanced educational programs anywhere on earth, but it is slowly turning away from curricula that are unrealistic and foreign to the experience of the African child and remote to the African context. Something of the feeling that Africans are developing toward their own educational institutions may be sensed from a remark by Dr. Aklilu Habte, former Dean of the Faculty of Education, Haile Selassie I University on the speaking and teaching of English. He said with some feeling, "We don't care so much about British English, or American English, or the English of India. We are concerned with Ethiopian English!"

Development of New Curriculum Materials

A decided trend in African education is the development of new curriculum materials that are "indigenous to African needs and relevant to African aspirations."[4]

This matter has been receiving attention from UNESCO, from U.S. AID educational advisors and university contract teams, from interested governments on both sides of the Iron Curtain, and from knowledgeable African educators. No one argues against the need. To learn to read English from primers depicting life in American suburbia, or to study a social studies transportation unit about the omnibuses of London doesn't particularly equate with the experiences of the African child. Consequently, although the

---

[3]M. Sequaries, "Traditional Teaching–Programmed Instruction," *African Education,* Vol. II, No. 1 (1964), 10-17.

[4]W. T. Martin, and J. L. Aldrich "The African Education Program Activities in Mathematics and Science," *ESI Quarterly Report* (Summer-Fall, 1967), 107-112.

developing nations have had to use any available course materials, they are now pushing hard to create, reproduce, and distribute their own curriculum materials.

The Entebbe mathematics series illustrates the new approach. During the summers of 1962, 1963, and 1964, six-week workshops were held at Entebbe, Uganda, and Mombasa, Kenya, in 1965. About sixty participants each year came from the United States, the United Kingdom, and from many sections of English-speaking Africa. According to the *ESI Quarterly Report*, the mathematics materials developed for pupils and teachers at both the primary and secondary levels were finding their way into at least ten African nations by 1965, including Ethiopia, Ghana, Kenya, Liberia, Malawai, Nigeria, Sierra Leone, Tanzania, Uganda, and Zambia. The materials were "designed to present in a systematic and logical manner, exciting to both students and teachers, some of the fundamental mathematical ideas and skills essential to a modern technologically-based society."[5]

Emphasis is given to the development of materials designed to create attitudes of respect and appreciation for national heritages. Although English customarily is taught in the elementary grades in English-speaking African countries, and is often the language of instruction in the secondary schools and above, attention is also being placed on the production of printed materials in the vernacular.

Organization

Let us now consider a number of other current educational aspects: organization, areas of action, problems, and some of the current trends.

First, we Americans should understand that the typical educational system in African countries is highly centralized. As a rule, there is a ministry of education that has general control and supervision of the national school system. Policies, regulations, and procedures normally originate in the ministry and are disseminated through the provinces to local schools. The same procedure usually applies to textbooks and instructional supplies.

---

[5]*Ibid.*, p. 108.

(Ethiopia typifies those nations where a significant portion of the funds for financing the schools comes from the central treasury. The country also has a local land tax for the support of rural and village elementary schools, but Addis Ababa and certain other provincial centers do not have city real estate taxes for school support.)

Centralization has its advantages, particularly in developing nations, but it also has its drawbacks. For example, not eighty miles from Addis Ababa one can see a well-constructed school building that was damaged by a heavy windstorm more than eighteen months previously. In spite of repeated requests, the local school authorities have not succeeded in getting funds to have even the broken windows replaced.

The government schools are sometimes organized on what we call an 8-4 basis, and sometimes on a 4-4-4 arrangement. Another common structure is the 6-2-4, with the lower grades being called the elementary or primary grades, grades 7 and 8 referred to as junior secondary, and the high school being called the senior secondary, or merely, the secondary school.

As might be expected, elementary schools are the most widely distributed; secondary schools are still limited mainly to the principal cities and provincial centers. The various national ministries of education are developing plans to increase the number of secondary schools, particularly by constructing facilities in remote areas where they do not now exist.

Teacher Education

Teacher-education programs are increasing in size and diversity, and are advancing to higher levels of preparation. Although many teachers who have not themselves completed elementary school may yet be found in the lower elementary grades, the trend is away from this situation. In Ethiopia, for example, most elementary school teachers now receive their preservice instruction in secondary level, elementary teacher-training schools. New junior-secondary teachers now are being required to complete a two-year college-level diploma course and the national university is striving to maintain the same academic standards required in lower-division degree courses. Ethiopia (which, incidentally, has hundreds of Peace Corps Volunteers teaching in its secondary schools) also requires its high school teachers to have degrees.

Progress is being made throughout the continent in raising the level of instructional ability of elementary teachers through in-service education. In addition to the correspondence courses provided, summer sessions for elementary teachers are being established. Ministry-sponsored, vacation-season educational opportunities are becoming available to teachers who have not completed secondary school, and a few colleges and universities are providing special post-secondary diploma programs during the off-season for elementary teachers who have previously completed high school. Not only are these teachers obtaining a better foundation in the content areas, but they are learning how to use locally available materials to enhance their instruction.

Modern concepts of supervision are being accepted. Recently trained supervisors are no longer defining supervision as inspection. They are viewing their duties as those of helping teachers to improve the quality of education. Consequently, teachers in some countries are receiving assistance in the performance of their work.

Literacy Campaigns

Government officials, educators, and other prominent citizens in the developing countries have recognized the importance of teaching reading and writing to all adults who are capable of learning. Consequently, government-encouraged and often government-sponsored literacy campaigns are a prominent feature of the new education in Africa. When one realizes that in some of the developing countries as few as 10 percent of the adult population can read and write, the need for these programs cannot be over emphasized.

These literacy campaigns are partly financed by government funds, but a large percentage of the needed money comes from private subscriptions. And, it is encouraging to note that educated youth are volunteering their services for these literacy programs. It is not unusual to find evening gatherings of adults, in whatever humble facilities may be available, under the tutelage of some alert, intelligent young man who is intent on giving them the great key to the storehouse of knowledge–literacy.

Unfortunately, there continues to be a decided lack of inexpensive reading material, and when the reading skill is not exercised, it begins to lapse. It is reported that in one area in the southern portion of the African Continent, vast quantities of printed communist propaganda were readily received by the newly literate to satisfy their craving for reading materials. To prevent this indoctrination, it has been suggested that action research be conducted in remote areas by following up literacy campaigns with small, locally produced newspapers, similar to the county newspapers that played such a vital role in the development of rural America. Here is a field of research and service for the journalist as well as the educator.

Education of Girls and Young Women

A noticeable trend in African education is the increasing inclusion of girls and young women in the schools and colleges. In many parts of the Near East and Africa, formal education for members of the female sex has not been considered essential; in fact, it has been regarded as a waste of time and money. Although this point of view has long since been discarded in many countries, it still persists in many rural areas of developing African nations. It is not unusual to visit classrooms, even in the elementary grades, where the ratio of boys to girls is about nine to one.

This picture, however, is changing—particularly in the cities and provincial centers; more and more girls are attending school. As a solid middle class develops along the lines of economic growth typical of western nations, parents realize the value of educating their daughters.

Furthermore, well-educated young men wish wives who have had some intellectual development. This is a matter of concern among single, male university students. They do not want to marry illiterate women, forseeing the problems in such marital unions. Nevertheless, with relatively few educated young women available, college educated men must turn to those who have had little opportunity for a formal education. (Of course, the above-described situation is not the only reason for the increase in school attendance by women.) The main point to keep in mind, however, is that for a variety of reasons, increasing percentages of young women are entering school and are staying on through the university.

Research and the Dissemination of Basic Scientific Knowledge

There has been a feeling on the part of many non-Africans that the emphasis in African higher education should be on the dissemination of basic scientific knowledge rather than upon complex research and technology. But, there are those in higher education on the continent who, while acknowledging the importance of the dissemination of knowledge, for various reasons (not excluding pride) want to see research progress simultaneously. They are experiencing considerable frustration because they do not have the funds, the facilities, or the personnel to establish a significant program.

Perhaps, more realistically, the needs of African education are: first, empirical research—more specifically, for applied research that will lead to the development and adaptation of educational methods, techniques, and materials now largely imported in toto from the western world; and second, for the invention of innovative instructional methods that build upon the many commendable aspects of local culture and attempt to harmonize (or at least not break too drastically) with the social setting from which the student comes.

The following example illustrates the adjustment problem an Ethiopian child faces when he attends school under the instruction of a Westerner—for example, a Peace Corps Volunteer. When called upon in class, the child speaks in a very low tone of voice and can barely be heard. The teacher insists that he speak up so that everyone may hear him; he is told of the importance of getting his message to others in the group. This may be most confusing to the younster for he has been taught at home that children should be seen and not heard. In fact, he has come to believe that it is rude for a child to speak up in the presence of adults. Furthermore, if he goes home and begins to practice speech habits that the Western teacher tries to instill in him, he will be in trouble with his parents. In addition, the parents will question what the school is doing to their child.

For reasons beyond their control African educators, even those who have been educated in Europe or the United States are not in a position to move forward rapidly in educational research and development. If significant advancement is to come in these areas, specific external assistance will need to be provided throughout the continent, with the possible exception of South Africa.

Problems

Formidable problems face the developing African nations in educational matters. Probably the problem of finance should be put in first place since, as was stated in a Rockefeller Brothers Fund report, "All the problems of the schools lead us back sooner or later to one basic problem–financing." These nations just don't have the money to do what needs to be done. This leads to the proverbial vicious circle, for without education the countries will not have the money to provide education.

Also, it is not feasible to push one segment of an economy too far ahead of the others. For example, commerce, industry, and agriculture need to be encouraged so that employment opportunities will be available to the student upon completion of his schooling. Conversely, these productive enterprises need educated employees if they are to progress. Therefore, the developing nations need to keep a balance between education and other developmental processes.

Other African education problems cannot be discussed fully in this limited space, but they include:

1. The need for qualified personnel, including teachers, administrators, and others that we call certificated personnel. (As R. M. Murray, Director, UNESCO Regional Center for Education in Africa once stated, "As there is never a lack of pupils, the yawning gap occurs always in the production of teachers."[6])
2. The shortage of buildings, furnishings, and equipment.
3. The paucity of instructional materials, whether foreign made or locally produced.
4. The progress lag due to traditions from colonial days and from the deeper-rooted past.
5. The high drop-out and force-out rates. (In Ethiopia, 45 percent of the first graders do not progress to Grade 2.)
6. The impatience with the rate of national progress on the part of the newly educated and those still in higher level schools. (It has been said that the expansion of education contributes directly toward instability, because it generates demands upon the political system which that system is unable to meet.)

Changes Necessary for Progress

Some of the demands of education in certain developing African nations have been discussed; selected ones are repeated below by way of review. Others not previously mentioned are also listed:

---

[6] R. M. Murray, "Training the Teachers of Youth and Adults in an Expanding Educational System," *African Education,* Vol. II, No. 2 (1964), 2-11.

1. For school curriculum experts to meet on an international basis to provide carefully formulated suggestions on curriculum reform and research.
2. To move away from passive memorization.
3. To organize the ministries of education along functional lines.
4. To upgrade the quality of administration.
5. To provide supervision in terms of the modern concept of working together to improve the total learning situation.
6. To seek minor decentralization of organization.
7. To expand the educational facilities and be able to give educational opportunities to all, even to the children of the nomads.
8. To encourage the official national languages as well as the teaching of English in English-speaking Africa.
9. To start community self-help school plant construction projects.
10. To provide "nationals" to teach in the secondary schools and at higher levels of education.
11. To preserve the best elements of national cultures and heritages even though this might risk preservation of some undesirable elements.
12. To produce local materials as instruction aids.
13. To examine and adapt to African conditions promising innovative educational developments from other parts of the world.
14. To experiment with the comprehensive high school concept and to give more attention to vocational education.
15. To focus attention upon the child as the center of concern.

Soviet Training Programs in Africa

It appears that penetration of Africa by the Soviet Union in educational affairs is somewhat concentrated in three areas, not to mention instruction in ideology, political theory, and philosophy. These areas are (a) training programs in the U.S.S.R. for persons from the African Continent, (b) study and research in the Soviet Union about Africa, and (c) vocational education programs in Africa, particularly those related to Soviet development projects on the continent.

The vocational preparation programs in Africa (as reported by the United States Office of Education) involve the construction of vocational technical schools or institutes and industrial facilities, and the training of African youth, primarily, but not exclusively, for work on development projects. As Seymour Rosen reported in 1963,

> The Soviet Union is involved in the construction of technical schools in the U.A.R., Guinea, Mali, Ethiopia and Somalia. Soviet technicians give African nationals on-the-job instruction in numerous industrial, transportation and

agricultural projects. A top Soviet official reported in October, 1961, that 5,000 specialists from the Soviet Union were working in countries that had become independent since World War II.[7]

Africa Needs Help in Educating Its Children

There is a growing feeling of accomplishment among African educators. Furthermore, a spirit of international cooperation is developing among them as means are being provided for them to meet in conferences, seminars, and workshops. This feeling was expressed by Dr. O. Ukeje of the Harden College of Education, University of Nigeria, when he wrote subsequent to the first Entebbe workshop:

> ... The Entebbe Mathematics Workshop is not only a project to make available new concepts and new methods in mathematics in African countries, but also it is to me an experiment in international cooperation, and a successful one at that. Here we have for the first time American professors and lecturers and teachers of mathematics—people from different nationalities, cultures and backgrounds working together harmoniously for the good of Africa and the progress of mankind. To me, and I am sure to most participants, the participation in this experiment has been an invaluable experience. I have personally learned a good deal, both in mathematics and in group cooperation; and I am sure others have done the same. It is indeed an experience which I think every participant will always remember and appreciate. Those who have made this experience possible can very well feel sure that they have made a remarkable contribution not only to the development of Africans and Africa, but also to the fostering of the brotherhood of mankind.[8]

This international cooperative spirit mentioned by Dr. Ukeje is essential. It is imperative that Africans and others work together. Assistance from highly developed countries must continue. Africa needs help in educating its children. The technical institute at Bahar Dar, Ethiopia, where the Blue Nile River heads at Lake Tana, is a good example of what is needed. The facility is a modern institution that would do credit to any country. If its operation is properly financed and administered, and if qualified instructional personnel can be obtained and retained, the school

---

[7] Seymour M. Rosen, *Soviet Training Programs For Africa.* (U.S. Department of Health, Education & Welfare, Office of Education, Bulletin 1964), No. 32 (OE 14108). Washington, D.C.: Government Printing Office, 1964.

[8] W. T. Martin, and J. L. Aldrich "The African Education Program Activities in Mathematics and Science," *ESI Quarterly Report* (Summer-Fall 1965), 112.

will make a significant contribution to that nation's development by providing desperately needed skilled workers and technicians. (Through the Agency for International Development and the Peace Corps, the United States is striving to prepare qualified instructors for institutions similar to the one at Bahar Dar.) An East African expression to the effect that "I don't have a donkey, so I don't have to worry about the hyenas" just will not apply to the situation the world faces today. The hyenas are lurking in the shadows; better defenses must be provided; problems must be solved.

If the humanitarian spirit of concern for others is the footing upon which lasting defense structures for mankind can be anchored, then education is the foundation that will overlay those footings and provide a base for the erection of enduring fortifications against the cunning, evil forces that would, like hyenas, dart in and snatch away freedom, leaving mankind enslaved. Many of us who have served in Africa are of the opinion that a strong foundation is now being laid, and if this progress continues, we shall see a far better Africa in a far better world. We look forward to the day!

Sino-Soviet Educational Relations

Stewart Fraser

Education in Communist China today is in a state of flux; a less generous commentator might describe it as chaotic and virtually anarchistic. Schools throughout China are held in abeyance; there have been enforced holidays for primary children for many months. A French press report from Peking, dated February 14, 1967, noted:

> Military Songs rang out in Peking primary schools today following reopening of the schools yesterday after they had been closed for six months.
>
> The reopening was ordered by the Communist party's Central Committee and the Government. Among the songs that the children were singing was "The Great Helmsman," dedicated to Chairman Mao. The youngest children, aged 7 to 9, are to be formed into groups of "little Red soldiers" in their classes. The curriculum includes study of quotations from Mr. Mao, ideograms and revolutionary songs, in that order.
>
> The return to school has caused relief among parents, who complained of the growing turbulence of youngsters overexcited by the revolutionary atmosphere in the streets. Their favorite sport has been to battle fiercely for leaflets thrown from windows by various Red Guards organizations.[1]

The rampages of the Red Guards and virtual disruption of all formal educational activities since June 1966 are well known by those who attempt to keep in touch with China. The "Great

---

[1] *Agence Presse*, Feb. 14, 1967.

Proletarian Cultural Revolution," spearheaded by high school student activists, has toppled many important Communist Party functionaries, not to mention various entrenched leaders in Peking. Throughout China, the "Cultural Revolution" has swept from office university presidents, school principals, and thousands of "unsatisfactory and stinkingly rotten" teachers. But at last, as a new Chinese year commences, there appears to be a modicum of sanity returning to the countryside. At least by early January 1967 reports from the provinces indicated that rural Communist Party officials had strongly requested that the primary schools for those in the six- to twelve-year-old group be permitted to reopen. The higher schools and universities do not seem to be ready for a new term immediately and probably they will not be fully reopened for another three or four months, or perhaps not until the autumn of 1967. (The higher schools and institutions are the spawning grounds for Red Guard activists, and until the present leaders of the "Cultural Revolution" have finished utilizing the services of the teen-agers, the educational activities of the high school will be of little interest to most of the students concerned.)

The internal troubles of China and the hiatus caused in the education of her youth have international ramifications. Overseas Chinese and foreign students arriving in or returning to China to commence the autumn term of 1966 had their studies "deferred." Many of the students have had to leave China and return to their homes in Africa and other parts of Asia. In addition, the few remaining Russian and other East European students have been "withdrawn" officially by their respective countries.

On both sides of the "taiga curtain" separating China and Russia there are disappointed students who will be unable to complete their studies or research. The remaining sixty-five or so Chinese students in the Soviet Union were recalled by Chinese educational authorities at the end of October or in early November 1966. The Soviet authorities stated that as early as September 20, the Chinese raised the question of cessation of training and educating Russians. In effect, they suggested that the students "clear out of China." Soviet authorities accordingly told their own students to return home by October 11. In addition, on October 7, they ordered the Chinese students to leave Russia "under the principle of reciprocity."

The U.S.S.R. allowed for the possibility of reinstating the student exchange programs in the future, however, but stated that "the Soviet side will be ready to consider the question of resuming on the basis of reciprocity, exchange of students, post-graduates, and trainees as soon as the Chinese display a readiness to resume such exchanges." But each side has accused the other of abrogating the cultural exchange agreement. Each places on the other the responsibility for causing the breach and for not taking initiative in overcoming the difficulties.

It is interesting to observe that the Chinese have not officially stated that Russian and other East European students were "expelled" from China. Instead, the following explanation, in paraphrased form, was given by the Chinese Communists:

> Because of the Great Proleterian Cultural Revolution, and the internal purges it necessitates in China, all classes have had to be suspended. Accordingly, foreign students cannot continue their research or studies and are being asked to go home for a year. In the case of the Soviet students, because they are at the end of their course of studies, they will be permitted to graduate early.

But graduate or not, they were not allowed to remain in China.

On Oct. 26, prior to their departure for home, the Chinese students in Moscow arranged for a salute to the memory of Lenin and Stalin. Press accounts of the Chinese students final pilgrimage into Red Square to pay their respects is amusing, if not ironic, in that they spent nearly four hours arguing and demonstrating before Soviet police would allow them to present and deposit the traditional wreaths that are a feature of such occasions. A press report (UPI, October 27, 1966) describing the behavior of the Chinese students noted:

> They had a hard time getting through a posse of red-faced Moscow policemen, but eventually they deposited their wreaths in Red Square and departed on a bus singing China's latest hit song, "The East is Red." The police, hearing the students were coming to pay their last respects to Lenin and their arch-hero, Stalin, quickly sealed off the square with barricades and boarded up the entrance to Lenin's huge granite mausoleum. "Closed for repairs," they shrugged when the bus-load of Chinese wearing Red Guard armbands, Mao Tse-tung lapel pins, and Maoist blue tunics arrived at the square and demanded entrance. "They want to make it a funeral procession," jibed Russian onlookers, as the Chinese students descended, carrying two six-foot wreaths of chrysanthemums, roses, and irises, argued with the adamant militiamen.

The police finally said the students could enter the square by bus. The students demanded to walk. Then they agreed to go by bus. But the police said they were being "capricious" and forbade entrance altogether. After about three hours of this, however, an agreement was reached. The students piled out of the bus with their badly wilted wreaths, posed for pictures, then got back on the bus and rode into the square. But the mausoleum remained closed, and to reach Stalin's tomb, the students had to go through it. Police refused to open up, but promised with a smile to "put the wreath where it belongs."

The Chinese laid their wreaths, one for Stalin, one for Lenin, in front of the mausoleum, and remained in a prayer-like attitude for about ten minutes. The good-natured Russian crowd, which had grown to about 300 persons, razzed the Chinese.

"Where are your purged leaders?" shouted one man. "Where are Molotov and Malenkov?" a Chinese shot back. "Why don't you cooperate with us in Vietnam?" someone in the crowd asked. "We don't want to be under the thumb of your foreign policy, which is in collusion with the United States," was the rejoinder. One Chinese youth shouted, "You cut off your aid to us and for awhile Peking had no buses." "So walk," hooted the crowd.

After laying their wreaths, the Chinese marched out of Red Square and re-boarded their bus. Then they opened the windows and started singing "The East is Red." Police ordered the bus to move on. It did–just around the corner, where the students began singing again. The police scowled. Eventually, the bus drove off, back to the Chinese embassy.[2]

The sixty-five or so Chinese students who had been studying in the Soviet Union were finally "repatriated" by Chinese authorities early in November 1966. The students who returned home by train via the Trans-Siberian Railway were given a tumultuous hero's welcome when they arrived in Peking. They spoke of the "indignities" heaped upon them by Soviet officials, but also mentioned the personal kindnesses of many Russian citizens. The Chinese noted dutifully the differences between official Soviet policy and the "traditional" friendship of the Russian and Chinese peoples. The temper and anger of the returning Chinese students have, of course, been matched by Soviet authorities, who also have raised various complaints against Chinese students and their political activities in Russian universities. Soviet educators are not reticent today in discussing their foreign student problems. Their

---

[2]*Nashville Tennessean*, Oct. 27, 1966.

comments on the intellectual capabilities of the Chinese students in Leningrad, Moscow, and Kiev have not been entirely ungenerous. The Russians have been sharply critical, however, of Chinese political "agit-propaganda" activities among university students and their participation in public demonstrations.

The tension in international education and cultural exchanges is obviously a reflection of other Sino-Soviet political differences, border disputes, the desire for leadership of world communism, and their interventionist but competing positions in Vietnam. The official educational and cultural exchange program between the U.S.S.R. and China has been terminated and, as noted above, the students have returned to their respective countries. Recent Soviet "good-will" visiting teams to China have had to curtail their visits and return home because of the unpleasant reception and even the personal violence they have encountered.

For several years it has been the practice for Peking and Moscow to exchange delegations to celebrate each other's national holiday, October 1 and November 7 respectively. The Russians received a Chinese delegation for the October celebration and followed protocol punctiliously, though perhaps frigidly. The Soviet delegation led by Viktor Mayevsky, a senior *Pravda* commentator, traveled to China in November for a two-week reciprocal visit. But by November 19 the Soviet delegation, which had been roundly insulted by their Chinese hosts throughout the visit (highlighted by "special effects" in Peking, Shanghai, and Canton), decided to return home and cancel the remainder of the "good-will" trip.

The leader of the delegation held a press conference in the Moscow House of Friendship on the group's return. It was reported by a staff correspondent of the *Christian Science Monitor* as follows:

> On November 7, the anniversary of the October Revolution, the delegation visited Peking University. "We heard neither congratulations nor statements about readiness to strengthen the friendship of our two countries," Mr. Mayevsky said. Instead, the Chinese attacked "Soviet revisionists." The delegation walked out of the hall.
>
> As they emerged into the courtyard, youthful Red Guards surrounded the delegation, "making it impossible for us to drive out. . . .We got out of the car and walked towards the gates of the university. A crowd of thugs

raged around us." "How could we respond to the outrages of the unbridled Red Guards?" Mr. Mayevsky asked. "The delegation decided to break into the organ-like tones of the international Communist anthem, the 'Internationale.'

"Then someone gave a command to the crowd which surrounded us to sing 'The East is Red.' For a tense moment the confrontation of songs continued: the first, a hymn-like appeal to the proletarians of the world; the second, an almost idolatrous glorification of Mao Tse-tung." Then representatives of the Sino-Soviet Friendship Society hurried up and hustled Mr. Mayevsky and his companions off the university campus. In Canton, a metropolis of south China where, in the mid-twenties, Soviet military and political advisers worked with Sun Yat Sen during the Nationalist-Communist alliance, the delegation met with new anti-Soviet statements.

A Chinese member of the Sino-Soviet Friendship Society made "the monstrous allegation that the Soviet Union had supposedly done China great harm." Then he said literally, "The Chinese people cannot forget or forgive that, just as the Soviet people cannot forget or forgive the crimes of the Hitlerite Fascists."

One of the Soviet delegation members, a party member since 1924, who had fought in World War II and had been made a Hero of the Soviet Union said: "Comparing us to Hitlerite Germany was so monstrous and incredible that I at first thought maybe this was a translation mistake. But it was deliberate." Indignantly, the Soviet delegation left the meeting amid insults and curses from the audience. One of their Chinese companions, a lady, shouted at them, "Cowards! Get out of here!"

Finally, on November 19, the delgation had to cut short its planned program and fly back to the Soviet Union. Mr. Mayevsky accused the Peking leadership not only of seeking to undermine Sino-Soviet friendships, but of "dreading like fire" any contacts between the two peoples. Soviet newspapers have hitherto carried many eyewitness accounts of the excesses of Peking's Mao-inspired "Great Proletarian Cultural Revolution." Mr. Mayevsky's report is not only the most detailed, but in a sense the most official, for he headed a delegation which went to China for the specific purpose of keeping alive Sino-Soviet friendship.

The prominence given by Soviet newspapers to the Mayevsky delegation's press conference shows the gravity with which the Kremlin regards the latest chapter in the steady disintegration of Sino-Soviet relations.[3]

It is of considerable interest to learn that the Chinese quickly went into print, published a vigorous rebuttal and attacked the Russians. The Chinese version of the disastrous Soviet-Chinese Friendship Tour is at considerable variance with the Russian account. It is quoted in full here to maintain historical accuracy:

---

[3]*Christian Science Monitor*, Nov. 1966.

Soviet Revisionists Turn Truth Upside Down in Anti-China Clamour

After creating an incident by unreasonably suspending the Soviet-Chinese Friendship Association delegation's visit to China, the Soviet revisionist leading clique has recently tried to foist the blame on China, using its propaganda machine to distort the facts and turn the truth upside down. It has made a big to-do of this incident in order to attack China. Kan Chi-min, Council Member of the Sino-Soviet Friendship Association, who accompanied the delegation throughout the time it was in China, has revealed the facts about the unreasonable suspension of the visit by the delegation and sternly refuted the slanders of the Soviet side.

Kang Chi-min said the delegation of the Soviet-Chinese Friendship Association led by Viktor Vasilievich Mayevsky, a Pravda commentator, came to China on November 2nd at the invitation of the Sino-Soviet Friendship Association to take part in the activities of the Chinese people celebrating the 49th anniversary of the Great October Socialist Revolution, and to pay a friendly visit in accordance with the 1966 cooperation plan between the two friendship associations. The Sino-Soviet Friendship Association and other institutions concerned follow the consistant teachings of the Chinese people's great leader, Chairman Mao, so, treasuring and safeguarding–as they always do–the friendship between the peoples of China and the Soviet Union, they gave warm and friendly hospitality to the Soviet delegation throughout its visit and did all they could to provide it with the best of facilities. During the delegation's brief visit of just 15 days, from November 2nd, the day it arrived, until November 17th, the day it unreasonably cut short its visit, the Chinese side arranged visits to Peking, Shanghai, and Kwangchow in accordance with the wishes of the delegation and after consultations by both sides. In Peking, the delegation attended the meeting in celebration of the 49th anniversary of the Great October Socialist Revolution. In Peking, and in other places, it visited four factories, two rural people's communes, four museums, two big exhibitions on achievments in industry and agriculture, in addition to visits to libraries, worker's cultural palaces, nurseries, and other places. In accordance with the requests of the delegation, the Chinese side arranged meetings for them with revolutionary students and teachers of colleges and middle schools, and Red Guards. They had discussions with Chinese writers and met activists of the Sino-Soviet Friendship Association. They also had wide contacts with thousands of Chinese workers, peasants, and people from all circles. Because of their profound friendship for the Soviet people, the Chinese people everywhere accorded the delegation the warmest welcome. When the Soviet delegation appeared for the first time in Tien An Men Square, a large group of Red Guards gathered around them. Many rushed forward to shake hands warmly and asked the Soviet guests to convey their best regards to the great Soviet people. During the visit to the Huang-tukang People's Commune, in the suburbs of Peking, the commune members cordially invited the delegation members to visit their homes. Some of them chatted with the commune members like old friends and they encouraged each other "to give the younger generation a good education and never to forget the past." In

Shanghai, a member of the delegation, a worker, was having a hearty talk with a Chinese worker and was reluctant to leave, but was pulled away by Mayevsky. These are iron-clad facts which Mayevsky can remember, as the events described were striking and quite recent. But when the delegation returned to the Soviet Union, Mayevsky talked utter nonsense. Distorting the facts, he said that as soon as the Soviet delegation arrived in China, it was "placed under extremely difficult conditions," and was "surrounded with an antagonistic atmosphere." In saying this, Mayevsky was trying to stir up anti-Chinese sentiments among the Soviet people.

Citing many facts, Kang Chi-min told how Mayevsky and his group on many occasions, picked quarrels and even openly interfered in China's internal affairs, and attacked China's great proletarian cultural revolution and foreign policy.

At a discussion with the Red Guards of higher educational institutions and middle schools in Peking, concerning the great cultural revolution in China, Mayevsky and his group asked them scores of questions, including many that were obviously very un-friendly. Though disapproving of the attitude of Mayevsky and his group, the Chinese Red Guards, treasuring the friendship between the peoples of China and the Soviet Union, nevertheless did all they could to restrain themselves and answered each question calmly. However, Mayevsky and certain other delegation members created an additional provocation when they openly slandered China's great cultural revolution by saying that it was "destroying culture" and "had no connection at all with the proletarian revolution." The Red Guards, their patience tried too far, refuted these statements by presenting the facts. Mayevsky then brazenly charged the Red Guards with being "anti-Soviet" and headed a demonstrative walk-out. He later lodged a most unreasonable "protest" with functionaries of the Sino-Soviet Friendship Association.

On the evening of November 7, the delegation attended the reception given by the Soviet Embassy in China to celebrate the 49th anniversary of the Great October Socialist Revolution. When the reception was over, several hundred revolutionary students and teachers and Red Guards from higher educational institutions in Peking spontaneously gathered on the road in front of the Peking Embassy to celebrate this glorious festival of the proletariat and the revolutionary people of the whole world. The Red Guard who presided over this gathering stated: "With feelings of infinite respect for the glorious October Revolution, boundless love for the great Soviet people, and immense indignation against modern revisionism, we warmly celebrate the 49th anniversary of the Great October Socialist Revolution." The Red Guards read out the message of greetings from the Central Committee of the Chinese Communist Party, the Standing Committee of the National People's Congress, and the State Council addressed to the Central Committee of the C.P.SU., the Presidium of the Supreme Soviet and the Council of Ministers of the Soviet Union. They cheered again and again: "Long live the Great Soviet People!"–"Long live the Unbreakable Friendship between the peoples of China and the Soviet Union!"–and "Down with Modern Revisionism!" This gathering, notable for the enormous revolutionary enthusiasm of the young Red Guard fighters, proceeded with great warmth and in perfect order. Mayevsky, however, ignored the facts and openly slandered the Chinese Red Guards as having "acted recklessly" and staged "anti-Soviet provocations" in front of the Soviet Embassy that evening.

After arriving in Shanghai from Peking to continue their visit, the delegates themselves declared that their tour of Shanghai was "satisfactory." But despite this, Mayevsky and his group again raised new issues and unreasonably demanded cancellation of the plan to visit the city of Changsha in central China the next day. They insisted on changing the scheduled route suddenly and wanted to go to Kwang-chow [Canton]. Great efforts were then made by the Chinese side to make these arrangements. But Mayevsky and other members of the delegation created more provocations during their visit.

On the day the delegation visited the 20th Chinese Export Commodities Fair in Kwang-chow, they were informed by their guide that China had established trade relations with more than 120 countries and regions in the world and that over 6,000 visitors from more than 60 countries and regions had visited that Fair; that both the number of visitors and the total of business transactions surpassed that of any of the previous fairs, and that this showed that "China has friends all over the world," and the policy of the imperialists headed by the United States to blockade and isolate China had gone bankrupt. On hearing these explanations, Mayevsky and his group not only did not rejoice in China's achievements in foreign trade, saying that it did "not conform to Marxist-Leninist principles." They voiced such nonsense as: Trade contacts between China and other countries on the basis of equality and mutual benefit "paralyse the will of the revolutionary peoples of the world." When these vicious attacks by Mayevsky and his group were denounced at the fair, they again took a demonstrative stance, staged a walk-out, and halted their visit. Following this, they made crude accusations to the Chinese side and unjustifiably and unilaterally decided to end their tour of China.

The delegation visited China at a time when all the Chinese students in the Soviet Union had unjustifiably been ordered to leave by the Soviet Government. The Chinese revolutionary masses and Red Guards, in their anger, lodged the strongest protests with the Soviet revisionist leading clique against their criminal act to deliberately strain Sino-Soviet relations. In this situation, Mayevsky and his group not only refused to examine their own activities, but on the contrary, misrepresented the Chinese people's opposition to the Soviet revisionist leading clique as "opposition to the Soviet people" and "anti-Soviet." They did this by standing the truth on its head and turning right into wrong. For such misrepresentation they repeatedly used the pretext that they had heard people shout in the streets "oppose modern revisionism with the leadership of the Soviet Communist Party as its centre" and other slogans, or saw posters such as "to oppose imperialism, it is imperative to oppose modern revisionism." Again and again without reason they lodged "protests" with the Chinese side.

Every time Mayevsky and his group created provocations, people from the Sino-Soviet Friendship Association who accompanied the delegation spoke with them repeatedly in the hope that they would cherish the friendship between the peoples of China and the Soviet Union, earnestly carry out the agreement between the friendship associations of the two countries, and complete their visit successfully so that the delegation would leave a good impression on the Chinese people. When the delegation wanted to end their visit, responsible members of the Sino-Soviet Friendship Association asked them many times to stay on. But Mayevsky and his group stubbornly rejected this advice. They continued to create provocations and act in an arbitrary manner. During their tour of China, on four occasions they left places in the middle of their visits; on four occasions they refused to carry out the arrangements made after consultations between both sides; on five occasions they lodged "protests" with the Chinese side without reason and twice issued statements threatening to terminate their whole visit. Finally, they went so far as to decide unilaterally and capriciously to end their visit and leave China ahead of schedule, thus creating an extremely bad precedent in the history of the exchange of visits between members of the friendship associations of China and the Soviet Union.

Kang Chi-min went on to describe how, after the Soviet-Chinese Friendship Association delegation returned home, the Soviet revisionist leading clique went even further. They encouraged Mayevsky to give a press conference to both Soviet and foreign correspondents in Moscow, issue vicious anti-Chinese statements, and spread lies through the TASS News Agency, the main Soviet newspapers, and the foreign press corps. They spuriously said that the delegation had been subjected to "anti-Soviet provocations," "attacks" and "abuse" in China, and "was obliged" to end its visit. This was an effort to mislead the Soviet people and the people of the whole world, so as to shift on to China their own criminal responsibility for sabotaging the agreement between the friendship associations of the two peoples.

At their press conference, Mayevsky and his group fabricated a flood of lies and made venomous anti-Chinese statements; they directed the spearhead of their attack against Chairman Mao Tse-tung, the great leader of the Chinese people and of the revolutionary people of the world. Ignoring the fact that the 700 million Chinese people and the revolutionary people of the whole world have a boundless love and esteem for their great leader, Chairman Mao, and for his philosophy, the Russian group went to all lengths in slandering the Chinese people's mass movement to study and apply Chairman Mao's works in a creative way as "the worship of a god." They failed to see the excellent situation existing in China's great proletarian cultural revolution and the acclamation for it by the world's revolutionary people, and even went to the extent of attacking that revolution as being "not a revolution" but as being "far away from" the interests of the workers and peasants, with one result being "the closing down of all the schools." They also tried to ignore the brilliant achievements of China's socialist construction, saying that there were "many difficulties" in China's industry and agriculture and that "the Chinese working class won state power only to perpetuate poverty."

Kang Chi-min emphasized that what Mayevsky and his group had done during their visit to China and on their return home fully demonstrated that the stopping of the visit by the delegation was a grave and premeditated anti-China incident organized and planned by the Soviet revisionist leading clique with the aim of further worsening Sino-Soviet relations and undermining the traditional friendship between the peoples of the two countries. They could not deny the countless iron-clad facts proving this.

Kang Chi-min said that the Soviet revisionist leading clique that has stepped into Khrushchov's shoes, in practicing Khrushchovism without Khrushchov, has been going farther and farther along the road of collusion with the United States in opposing China. They have sunk to the lowest depths in their attempt to whip up a new anti-China wave, to curry favor with U. S. imperialism, and to realize their dream of so-called "Soviet-U. S. cooperation for world domination." Our great leader, Chairman Mao, has said that people like this "started with the aim of injuring others only to end up ruining themselves. This is the law of development which governs all reactionary policies." The Soviet revisionist leading clique which is engaged in all kinds of vile activity, will ultimately be overthrown by the Soviet people.

In conclusion, Kang Chi-min said that the 700 million Chinese people, taught by our great leader, Chairman Mao, and the Chinese Communist Party, will be friends always with the Soviet people, who have been nurtured by the great Lenin. The friendship between the Chinese and Soviet people is eternal and cannot be disrupted by anyone. The anti-China clamour of the Soviet revisionist leading clique and its flunkeys is not more than a dark spot on the face of the sun, it can never blot out the radiance of the great friendship between the Chinese and the Soviet peoples.[4]

The present state of affairs is in extreme contrast to the situation of a decade ago when Sino-Soviet educational and cultural exchanges were at their height. More than fourteen thousand Chinese students received an education in the Soviet Union during the period of the various exchange programs. The text of China's first Five-Year-Plan, released in 1956, noted:

The sending of students abroad to study or to get practical training is an important measure for raising our general scientific and technical level and improving the management of enterprises in our country. In this five-year period, 10,100 students will be sent abroad to study; 9,400 of them will go to the Soviet Union and 700 to the People's Democracies and other countries.[5]

---

[4]"Soviet Revisionists Turn Truth Upside Down in Anti-China Clamour," *Peking Review*, Vol. 9, No. 52 Dec. 23, 1966, 28-30.

[5]Stewart Fraser, "Sino-Soviet Educational Cooperation: 1950-1960," *Government Policy and International Education* p. 199. (New York: John Wiley and Sons, 1965).

At the height of the program in 1959-60, more than three thousand Chinese students were studying in the Soviet Union. An augmented and specialist advisory staff was necessary to counsel and to administer the enormous program in the Chinese Embassy in Moscow. As early as 1957, when the program was fast developing, there were some startling self-critical comments from Chinese who, under the temporary "Free Speech Movement" of "blooming and contending," attacked the program. A senior educational administrator in Peking stated that:

> There is a tendency for political qualifications to override the cultural and technical qualifications. Many students sent to Soviet Russia find difficulty in keeping up with their studies. . . .The stock of the student who has been to Russia rises sky high on his return. He gets a cushy job and a princely salary and enjoys all sorts of privileges, including meals, special messes, without having to prove his worthiness.[6]

Of course this situation may not have changed in its entirety, especially if the "returned Chinese student" was forcibly ejected from the Soviet Union. Undoubtedly this distinction could be of political importance and will be for many students a reminder of the "perfidious" nature of the Russian foreign student program. With the return of the last group of Chinese students in November 1966 the collapse of the program now appears to be final.

Up to this time it has been difficult to obtain documentary evidence and useful statements concerning Sino-Soviet educational relationships during the past months. It is clear, however, that detailed and obviously vitriolic analyses and statements will be forthcoming in the near future from the Chinese, and possibly from Russian sources, also.

In conclusion of this report, therefore, a document is reproduced which should be of unique value in illustrating the all-time low that Sino-Soviet relations have reached in the field of international educational exchange. This extensive statement was taken from a monitored radio broadcast from Peking issued by the New China News Agency on November 5, 1966. A returned Chinese student, Hung Kang, angrily accused Soviet officials and educators of persecuting Chinese students in Russia. She addressed a Peking rally to welcome home Chinese students expelled by the Soviet Union. Excerpts of her speech are presented here:

---

[6]*Ibid.*, p. 200.

The Soviet revisionist leading clique has always sabotaged the cultural agreement between the two countries. Either it intentionally posponed arrangements for the studies of the Chinese students for a long period or it violated the agreement by altering their specialties without consultation.

It has never guaranteed or provided adequate conditions for the studies of the Chinese students. It has always created excuses to arbitrarily shorten their period of study. It forced students to suspend their studies, racked its brains, and did everything in its power to sabotage the agreement.

As a result of the intentional delay on the part of the Soviet side in making arrangements for his studies, post-graduate student Hu Te-pao who went to the Soviet Union in August last year (1965), did not even begin his studies in all his fourteen months and more in the Soviet Union. On the eve of his departure from Moscow for home, a foreign friend told him with indignation: "You have finished your studies before they were started."

Teacher Chang Hung-pin went to Moscow University last year (1965), with the agreement of the Soviet side, for advanced study in the analysis and separation of isotopes. But when he arrived in Moscow the Soviet side changed its mind on the pretext that Moscow University had no such specialty. Later they created another excuse that the man in charge of the specialty was soon to go abroad, although he did not in fact go abroad until more than a year later. Obstructed by the Soviet side, Chang Hung-pin had no alternative but to change his specialty.

Most of the Chinese students who went to the Soviet Union last year were placed by the Soviet side in cities and schools with very poor conditions for study. The schools lacked facilities for study; moreover, most of them had never received any foreign students before, and the teachers were incompetent and inexperienced.

The Soviet side did not provide the Chinese students with the necessary conditions for study; what is more, they did their utmost to create difficulties for studying. They placed 25 Chinese students taking advanced studies in practical Russian in Irkutsk, Siberia, because they were fearful of their propagating Mao Tse-tung's thought in Moscow, the center of revisionism. In Irkutsk, these Chinese students had none of the necessary facilities for studying the language; even the minimum necessity—a classroom—was not guaranteed.

A Chinese postgraduate student who studied in the Electro-Chemistry Research Institute of the Soviet Union was refused permission to visit laboratories related to his study, although the Soviet side allowed Americans to visit them freely. The Chinese students were denied the opportunity to carry out field demonstrations, although the Soviet side made arrangements for Soviet students and students from other countries.

We Chinse students, brought up by the party and Chairman Mao, always love labor, are diligent, and live frugally and simply, never worrying about living conditions or personal gain. However, we cannot but be indignant about the discrimination and persecution to which the Chinese students were subjected by the Soviet revisionists in the arrangements for our living.

Last year, one of our fellow students, who had just arrived in the Soviet Union, was assigned to live in a very dilapidated hut designed for three people. Later, when it was learned that someone from the Chinese Embassy was going to see him, he was hurriedly moved to a hotel. A promise was given to accommodate him in a newly-built dormitory. But up to last July, when all the other research students were accommodated in decent-sized rooms, the Chinese student's lodging problem was left unsolved.

Still more intolerable was the treatment of two Chinese students from Sinkiang, Mumin and Mansuri, who were studying in Tashkent. After the first earthquake in Tashkent, all the foreign and Soviet students living with the Chinese students were moved to places of safety. Only the Chinese students were left to stay on in the old place. The Soviet authorities brazenly said: "You are already in the fifth year. The others are first-year students. It would be a serious loss if they were killed." It was not until a month later, after the Chinese students had lodged four protests, that they were allowed to move.

The new Soviet revisionist leadership has always regarded the Chinese students as its greatest political enemy. They have consistently pursued a savage and fascist-like persecution of the Chinese students. They constantly had agents watching our actions, secretly listening to or making tape recordings of our conversations, and secretly examining our books and study material. They forbade Chinese students to receive guests, forbade Soviet people and even Chinese residents in the Soviet Union to have contact with the Chinese students, sent thugs to prevent Chinese students from listening in to Peking radio, and unjustifiably prevented the Chinese students from receiving copies of the Peking *Peoples' Daily* to which they subscribed. The Chinese students in Kharkov, who subscribed for a year of *Peoples' Daily* at the Soviet postoffice, received in all not more than a month's copies of the paper.

This is not all; incidents constantly occurred in which, under one pretext or another, Chinese students were subjected to violence and bloodshed. On March 4 last year (1965) Chinese students spilled their blood on the streets of Moscow when they took part in the foreign students' demonstration to support Vietnam and oppose U. S. imperialism, and they were cruelly suppressed by the Soviet authorities. The Soviet authorities also sent thugs to throw mercury, cigarette butts, or boxes of matches into the Chinese students' cooking pots, and beat them up in the middle of the night when they were asleep. Although we demanded time and again that the Soviet authorities should undertake to guard the safety of Chinese students, the persecution of them, far from being reduced, became more flagrant and outrageous.

On October 10, 1966, an anti-China lecture was given at Leningrad University. When three Chinese students asked to speak, a group of agents and thugs rushed onto the rostrum, surrounded the three Chinese students separately and beat them up.

On China's National Day it has been the custom for Chinese students to celebrate the occasion by telling Soviet teachers and students about the great achievements of China's socialist revolution and socialist construction. At the 17th anniversary of New China last October 1, the Chinese students as usual applied to give a small pictorial exhibit for the occasion. But, with a few exceptions, the Chinese students' reasonable requests were turned down by the Soviet authorities in charge because they were afraid of the truth, afraid of the thought of Mao Tse-tung, and afraid that the Soviet masses would become informed of China's real situation. When the Chinese students asked why the Chinese were denied the right to hold an exhibit, while the United States was allowed to do so in Moscow, the answer was: "It's because the United States does not oppose us." This indeed was a self-revelation. This was a truthful confession of Soviet alignment with the United States to oppose China.

With a despicable political aim in mind, the Soviet revisionist leadership even resorted to the use of "sugar-coated bullets" to corrupt the Chinese students studying there, who were armed with Mao Tse-tung's thought, in a vain effort to tempt them and bring about their "peaceful evolution."

Still more outrageous is the fact that the Soviet Government, after unilaterally tearing to pieces the agreement on cultural cooperation between the two countries by ordering the Chinese students to suspend their studies, went so far as to instruct Soviet Communist Party members to incite a revolt of the Chinese students.

At Irkutsk University, a Soviet Communist Party member even came openly to the Chinese students on a number of occasions and attempted to delude them into betraying their motherland. He had the impudence to make the despicable suggestion: "If you want to ask for political asylum, you need do nothing more than sign a paper." When the Chinese students angrily asked him who sent him, this person promptly confessed: "It's not my own idea; it was decided in consultation."

When the revisionists failed to wear their false, smiling masks, their true fascist-type features appeared. The revisionist authorities of Tashkent attempted to conceal from the Chinese students the Soviet Government's unjustified decision to suspend their studies and plotted to detain a Chinese student, Mu Ming, secretly. When Mu Ming received a note from the Chinese Embassy and was about to leave Tashkent for Moscow, those stupid fellows sent policemen and thugs to seize Mu Ming's luggage. They seriously injured his arm. Failing to attain their objective by force, they tried to prevent the Chinese student from catching the train on the pretext that his luggage was overweight. Through the valiant struggle of Mu Ming and the help of revolutionary African classmates, this plot of the revisionists went bankrupt in the end.

The revolutionary spirit and the good idealogical style of the Chinese students won high tribute and left a deep impression on the minds of the ordinary people of the Soviet Union. Many Soviet students and others said to us: "It is Comrade Mao Tse-tung who trains you all so well." One teacher said: "I have been teaching for more than ten years, but never have I taught such good students as you. I would be very willing to go on studying with you and teaching you. But I cannot help myself."

The grave step taken by the Soviet revisionist leading clique in ordering all Chinese students in the Soviet Union home was a long-contemplated act. A Soviet communist told us: "Before 30 September (1966), the Central Committee of the CPSU had already notified its basic organizations that all of you would be ordered home. You will not return."

Our great teacher, Chairman Mao, said: "Lifting a rock only to drop it on one's feet is a Chinese folk saying to describe the behavior of certain fools. The reactionaries in all countries are fools of this kind. In the final analysis, their persecution of the revolutionary people only serves to accelerate the people's revolutions on a broader and more intensive scale." This is exactly how things have taken place.

We are profoundly impressed by the fact that the Soviet people are always on our side. They showed immense indignation at the Soviet revisionist leading clique's act, which is intended to undermine Sino-Soviet relations and the friendship between the Chinese and Soviet people by driving out the Chinese students from the Soviet Union. This time when we bade farewell to them, many parted with tears in their eyes. One of them said: "Don't forget, please, the Soviet people are friendly toward you. This evil thing is done only by the leaders." A Soviet teacher told some Chinese students: "These new leaders have never done a single good thing for Sino-Soviet relations. As a Soviet citizen and a rank-and-file Soviet Communist Party member, I feel ashamed of their foolish behavior. We Soviet people want to be friendly with the Chinese people"

The Soviet revisionists have done every evil thing. Their days are numbered. The day is coming when the Soviet people will rise to their feet to overthrow them and put them on trial.[7]

---

[7]"Soviet Revisionist Renegades Obstruction and Persecution Against Chinese Students," *Peking Review*, Vol. 9, No. 45, Nov. 25, 1966, 25-57.

The Challenge to Higher Education in India

Anoop C. Chandola

From any point of view, India is one of the most diverse countries in the world. As different races have continually entered and settled there, it has been the melting pot of humanity since time immemorial. One of the most interesting characteristics of Indian culture is its ability to maintain its own individuality in addition to its many different subcultures. Within its borders, India has representatives of all the major races of humanity, all of the major religions of the world, and hundreds of diverse languages. India is really a curry-powder nation made up of all sorts of spices. Indians love this diversity as they love their curry powder; but then it is not always easy to make a really good curry. If India succeeds in making a really good curry with secular democracy as its fuel, there is hope that the entire world, with all kinds of people, can live and work together no matter how many differences—natural or man-made—there may be among them.

There are two serious problems confronting India today—education and economic standards. Would you believe that 60 percent of the people in the country that invented numerals cannot read numerals? Would you believe that 60 percent of the people cannot read and write the alphabet in the country that invented the science of phonetics? Would you believe that a country that had universities hundreds of years ago is today unable to solve some simple problems of higher education? Such a country is India, whose population is estimated to be 500 million people. We will never be able to count the Indians, however, because by the time this sentence is finished, another baby will have been born in that land.

India is not worried about how to reach the moon; she cannot afford such a worry. Her people are not even worried seriously whether they should have communism or capitalism. India *is* worried about her bare survival on this planet, Earth. The current economic and political plight of the nation is blamed on the period of foreign domination lasting 150 years. It was thought that after independence India would emerge as a modern nation; but when the day of independence came on August 15, 1947, it was not a happy day for most Indians. India was partitioned into two countries; India and Pakistan. Thousands of innocent people were sacrificed on the altar of political rites to satisfy the ambitions of some political leaders. More than 60 percent of the Indians who had been living peacefully with animals (being vegetarians) discovered they could not live in peace with each other.

In planning for independence, the Indian leaders recognized the fact that if India was to become a modern and progressive nation, then religion should not be mixed with politics. In November, 1947, the concept of the "secular" nation was noted in the Indian Constitution. The entire educational policy of India is oriented toward such a goal today, and those who study Indian education recognize that a new generation has accepted the policy of separating church and state.

According to the Directive Principle of the Indian Constitution, all children between the ages of six to fourteen were supposed to have universal, free, and compulsory education. This goal has not been achieved, mainly because of the unexpected population explosion. However, today more than 80 percent of the children between the ages of six and eleven are in schools. There were 265,844 college students in 1947. This number had increased to 1,528,227 by 1965. There were sixty-two universities in 1965 compared with twenty in 1947. In the year 1964-65, there were 2,360 colleges in India. There were 6,682 higher secondary schools in 1949-50. In 1960-61, this figure rose to 17,226 and the estimated number for 1966 is 24,000. As a result of the increase in educational institutions, the literacy rate was 24 percent in 1961 as opposed to 17 percent in 1947, and at the present time, it is estimated to be over 40 percent. As far as literacy is concerned, India has made a tremendous leap in a very short period of time.

Recent elections are a good indication of the success of the literacy program. An analysis of this election indicates concrete examples of the secularization of the voters. Voters cast their ballots for the man, not for the party, caste, community, or religion. For example, in some predominantly Muslim areas, Hindu candidates won, and similarly, in some predominantly Hindu areas, the Muslim candidates won. It was also noticed that some candidates won election in their non-native regions over other candidates who were natives of the area. We can safely conclude that today the people of India have become more politically conscious than at any time during the past century.

With the exception of four universities that are directly connected with the central government, education in India is the responsibility of the state governments. An Act passed by either the Indian National Parliament at New Delhi or one of the state legislatures may establish a university. The central government or state government has a Ministry of Education directed by an Education Minister. It is the job of the Education Ministry to look after all problems of education at all levels. The governor, as the head of the state, is also chancellor of the state universities. In the case of the four central universities, either the President or the Prime Minister of India acts as chancellor. The position of chancellor is ceremonial, but at times he can exercise considerable influence in various affairs of the university. The top executive of the university is the vice-chancellor and is the equivalent to the president of an American university. He is assisted by an executive committee of the university, called the Syndicate or the Executive Council. There is an Academic Council as well that is responsible for the academic functions of the university. The highest body of the university is known as the Senate or the Court. This Senate consists of the representatives of teachers, alumni, government, and the local community.

There are seventy universities in India. These universities fall into three catagories: (1) residential and teaching; (2) affiliating;

(3) affiliating and teaching. A residential and teaching university usually includes all faculties and colleges in one single place. Such a university is similar to the pattern observed at Harvard, Yale, or the University of Chicago. Affiliating universities consist of several colleges in different places, each college having its own teaching and research faculties. All of the curricula, courses, examinations, and diplomas of these colleges, however, are the responsibility of one single organization. This organization does not offer any teaching and research; it is simply an administrative body. The affiliating and teaching type of university also consists of several colleges; each college has its own faculties that provide teaching up to the bachelor's, and sometimes to the master's degree. Teaching and research leading to master's and Ph.D. degrees are conducted at one place for which there is only one single organization.

Most of the younger universities are of the residential type and have faculties for teaching arts, sciences, commerce, and engineering; few have faculties for teaching in the areas of medicine and agriculture. A few universities are highly specialized, e.g., Roorkee University for engineering, and U. P. Agricultural University. There are some other institutions deemed universities; for example, Gurukul Kangari Vishwasvidyalaya at Hardwar, which is modeled after the ancient Indian educational system. A very few new institutes have been modeled after the California Institute of Technology or the Massachusetts Institute of Technology.

Normally, after one completes what is known as "higher secondary school," a bachelor's degree requires an additional four years of college work, with another two years required for the master's degree. (In technology and in medicine, the number of years necessary to earn a bachelor's degree is considerably more. The number of years, however, varies from university to university.)

The foundations of the present educational system (with the exception of a few peripheral institutional systems) were laid down by the British. As early as 1792, the British were interested in educating the Indians, but there was opposition by members of the Court of Directors who opposed resolutions to educate Indians with the statement that "they [the British] had just lost America because of the folly of having allowed the establishment of schools and colleges, and it would not do for them to repeat this error in regard to India." In 1835, it was Lord Macaulay, then a member of the executive council of the Governor-General of India who was the first to give serious thought to the education of Indians through the British system. Macaulay stated the objective of this British type of education as: "We must do our best to form a class who may be interpreters between us and the millions whom we govern; a class of persons Indian in blood and color but English in taste, in opinions, in morals, and in intellect." Indians, of course, have considered these words offensive, but at the same time they cannot forget that Macaulay also said in the House of Commons: "Are we to keep the people of India ignorant in order that we may keep them submissive? Or do we mean to awaken ambition and to provide it with no legitimate vent? It may be that the public mind of India may expand under our system until it has outgrown that system, that by good government we may educate our subjects into a capacity for better government, that having become instructed in European knowledge, they may in some future age demand European institutions. Whether such a day will ever come, I know not. Whenever it comes, it will be the proudest day in English history. The sceptre may pass away from us. Victory may be inconstant to our arms. But there are triumphs which are followed by no reverses. There is an empire exempt from all natural causes of decay. These triumphs are the pacific triumphs of reasons over barbarism." Certainly these words deserve much praise.

Raja Rammohun Roy, the famous Indian reformer, also favored the British type of education. The Governor-General, Lord William Bentinck, accepted Macaulay's recommendations. At that time only higher education was considered important, and primary or secondary education was ignored completely. Financial support was given only to colleges teaching in the British system where the English language was used exclusively. The native Indian languages were especially ignored as a medium of instruction.

In less than twenty years, it became apparent that western knowledge did not reach the masses. In 1854, Sir Charles Wood proposed to the Court of Directors that a comprehensive plan be made for the establishment of primary, secondary, and high schools, in addition to colleges and universities, which would be the vehicle for the spread of western arts, science, philosophy, and literature. There were other recommendations made at that time—such as divorcing education from religious connotations, accepting Indian languages in addition to English as the media of instruction, and making government aid available to private schools if they would submit to government inspection.

Following these recommendations, in 1857 universities were established in three big cities: Calcutta, Bombay, and Madras. These three universities were similar to the University of London in their administrative and academic character. Subsequently, other universities came into existence based on the British pattern. In retrospect one can evaluate the good and the bad points of Sir Charles Wood's recommendations. For example, secular education and recognition of the native languages at some levels were undoubtedly worthwhile. Too much emphasis on western education, government inspection, and governmental control by financial aid were some of the weaker points. Even today, although India has achieved independence from British rule, these less desirable aspects prevail in Indian higher education.

There have been several educational reforms during the years, but they have not brought any tangible success. Indian universities are essentially nothing but dim carbon copies of British universities, unsuitable to the Indian environment. The serious problems that confront Indian higher education have been generally ignored by the governments of India, as well as by the educators themselves.

Essentially, most of the plaguing problems of higher education in India center around the problem of "communication." Successful communication between teacher and student is the most important criterion for evaluating any educational system. The main means of communication is language. In India, there are fourteen constitutional languages, and each of these languages is used in a particular state or states. Some of these languages are not spoken by more than eight or nine percent of the Indian population. But because of over-enthusiasm for democracy, the Indian government tries to please all sections of the country. India is the only country where fanaticism and ignorance make it possible for one and the same language to be recognized as two different ones merely because it is written in two scripts–Hindi and Urdu are only one language, but if one writes it in Perso-Arabic script it is Urdu and if it is written in Nagari script it is Hindi. The seventeen states of India are formed basically by the criterion of language. Multilinguism has created serious difficulties for the entire nation and regionalism based on regional language has threatened national integrity. In order to preserve the national unity, India has adopted a three-language formula. According to this formula, every student must learn three languages: Hindi, English, and one regional language. Perhaps this formula is the only solution, and after thirty or forty years there may not be a problem of mass communication in India.

Higher education suffers from another problem: up to higher secondary education, the medium of instruction is one of the Indian languages. The universities are free to adopt English or Hindi or any regional language as their medium of instruction. Thus, some universities have English as the sole medium of instruction; others have two coexisting media of instruction. Some subjects like medicine and engineering are taught in English at all the institutions.

One may wonder why some Indian universities switch to non-English languages. There are two extreme opinions in India concerning the language of instruction. One opinion holds that all education must be imparted through the mother tongue of the student. Many educators might agree on this point, and certainly things are more intelligible when explained in the mother tongue. But in India, the group that holds this opinion wants to eliminate all foreign words, especially technical words, from the Indian languages. Unfortunately, this group has been more powerful than any other. Consequently, today there are huge translation projects sponsored by both central and state governments, as well as by private organizations. These projects have been established to coin a Sanskrit word for a corresponding foreign word. The position of Sanskrit in India is very like that of classical Greek and Latin in modern Europe. Few Europeans can read Greek and Latin. If a technical name is needed for a new concept, however, it might be coined from classical Greek or Latin. Sanskrit, therefore, dead as a spoken language for hundreds of years, is the Indian counterpart of classical Greek and Latin. Many are disappointed to know that there are educated people in India who want to make Sanskrit the official national language. I do not wish to imply that we should ignore Sanskritic studies, but one does not make a dead language an official language simply because he wishes to say, "This is the mother tongue." Essentially, we cannot reincarnate dead languages. When one can accept the foreign concept implicit in a technical word, clearly noted, what difference does it make which language is being used?

We must remember that language is a structure. It is the grammatical structure of the language with which the child is reared. The child will grasp this structure. Every language has the ability to integrate the loan-words from another language without changing the grammatical structure. Thus, as long as the structure is not changed, one cannot say that the language is changed. Every loan-word has a structural slot in the borrowing language. So long as the loan-word is in its structural slot of the language there cannot be any problem with its usage. Of course, as far as the usage of a technical word is concerned, it has to be explained no matter if the word is on loan or a native vocable, for a technical word is not in itself self-explanatory. For example, the word "telephone" is Greek, and the English borrowed it. Suppose one changes it to "far-sound" and discards the foreign word "telephone" from the English language. Will the English-speaking student understand the mechanism of "telephone" simply because his native word "far-sound" exists instead of the Greek word, "telephone"? The student will understand it only when it is demonstrated by its mechanism and explained in his mother tongue. What is meant here is to note that the mere translation of a loan-word will not facilitate teaching. By translating the word "telephone" into Hindi, the concept or the soul of the word will always remain foreign because the Indians did not invent telephone. Thus, the effort for acquiring a false dignity is a kind of self-deception.

Let us note, therefore, the damage that the policy of translating technical words into Sanskrit has done to education in India. As mentioned, some Indian universities have retained English as the sole medium of instruction; others have not. The greatest problem comes, therefore, when a student wants to transfer from one university to another. He might have been taught in a native language that did not use foreign loan-words. Now he enters a university where English is the medium of instruction. Imagine how much time and energy this student will waste in the switchover of a huge technical vocabulary. Thus, the student is handicapped because of a language problem within his own country.

Suppose a student from Gujarat University in the western region of India where Gujarati is also the medium of instruction, goes to Lucknow University in the north where Hindi is the medium of instruction. Here Hindi and Gujarati have not been using common terminology, and sometimes there are several words for a loan in the same language. The student has a tremendous difficulty in adjusting to the new medium. This language barrier is discouraging to the mobility of the students. And since the young generation in India is not mobile, national integration will be a continuing problem.

Associated with the problem of language are problems relating to textbooks. Teachers, and others, have been encouraged to translate English textbooks into Hindi, or into other Indian languages authorized for specific fields of study. In spite of this encouragement, there are tremendous shortages of translated school textbooks. Therefore, while the students are required to read English textbooks, they must answer questions and hold discussions in Hindi, because Hindi is the medium of instruction in that field. In such a pattern, academic standards have diminished. The teacher in chemistry, for example, fails to translate all of the technical words. The examiner, who is from another university, expects the students to use translations in the examination. Students cannot always succeed, and thus they suffer at the hands of an external examiner who is not aware of the limitations imposed by a particular university. Even if there are sufficient textbooks, the Indian students cannot profit from current research publications in foreign languages, such as English, German, French, and Russian, as there is simply no formal arrangement for translation. A few universities have a well-developed program in those foreign languages important for scientific scholarship, but this is not general. Foreign language instruction, including the teaching of English, is highly defective because it is not based on any principle of applied linguistics. The "language experts" in India are those who may not possess even an elementary knowledge of modern linguistics.

Another problem confronting higher education in India concerns the environment; more specifically, we might say the environment for communication. It has been said that the teachers in India are not equipped with adequate knowledge, and that the students graduating from Indian universities are inferior to the students produced by western universities. This is probably true and especially so in the sciences, technological fields, and medicine. Much has been said about this by those who are concerned, and the question may be posed as follows: Can a university teacher communicate to his students what he knows and what he wants to communicate? Some teachers are not very successful in communication or teaching methods. One of the main reasons is a lack of discipline within the classrooms. Although many suggestions have been given concerning ways to improve classroom discipline, undoubtedly the basic cause of disciplinary problems is the high student-teacher ratio. It is not uncommon for some of the classes in India to enroll between three and four hundred students. Loudspeakers are used throughout a large classroom. Thus, there is no personal contact between the teacher and students, and certainly not in any communicative sense.

Indian students frequently indulge in strikes, riots, and other destructive activities. As there is only one examination at the end of the academic year, no daily assignments, and no weekly, monthly, or mid-term examinations, the student has plenty of time to waste if he so wishes.

There are some academic fields wherein experiments in the laboratories are compulsory, and in these areas, perhaps, the students are more serious about their studies. Most of the universities have adopted tutorial systems in name only, and although such a system should afford more assignments and examinations for students, they are not possible in the large classes. Further, the students know that their teachers will not be their examiners. A student knows that the opinion of the teacher about him and his work will in no way relate to his final examination or grade. So the student does not respect the teacher. No matter how much respect Indian ancestors may have given to the teacher (a Sanskrit saying is that "Guru is the very God"), such respect is not observed today. The teacher is sometimes considered to be a paid teaching servant of the students.

Undoubtedly, there are many solutions to the problem of discipline in India, but certainly the present system of teaching and evaluating the students' progress needs to be revised. Several examinations should be given during any course offered, and each such examination should be considered in any final grade given to the student. Most important, the teacher alone should examine his student. Currently, the position of examiner is a great business in India, and open only to a few lucky teachers. One examiner may grade hundreds of answer books from several different schools. A huge amount of money is spent in organizing and printing these question papers and answer books, and in paying travel expenses for those who are involved in the process. This money could be more effectively spent in raising the salary of the teachers and providing tuition scholarships and fellowships for students.

Some educators believe that a teacher may be prejudiced about his students for non-academic reasons, and this of course is always possible, It is also possible that the teachers might be approached and bribed by parents of the students. It must be observed, however, that the teacher-student relationship has developed into a wholesome partnership in the western culture. Certainly the validity of an evaluation based on no contact at all with the student is questionable.

Another problem of higher education in India concerns the mass production of graduates. The simple fact is that India does not need as many graduates, specifically in the humanities (languages, literature, history, politics, and philosophy,), the social sciences (anthropology and sociology) and commerce as are being produced. One reads in the newspapers that thousands of Indian graduates are unemployed. Actually, even those who do become employed do not obtain the kind of work they like or perhaps deserve. For example, a Ph.D. in Sanskrit may teach in a secondary school not only in his major area, but also in several other areas, such as mathematics, history, and geography, for a salary of twenty dollars a month. A person with a master's degree in political science may be found as a clerk in a local cloth mill, and so on. A student who has received a bachelor's degree does not want to accept a job requiring physical labor. Instead, he prefers to remain unemployed, and thus continues to be an economic burden.

More than 50 percent of the candidates for a diploma fail in final examinations. The students can repeat these examinations any number of times. A student who takes a diploma is classified in one of three catagories called "divisions" or "classes," namely,

First, Second, and Third, which roughly correspond to A-, B-, and C- averages in an American university. The entire system has led to an overproduction of graduates. One way, of course, to stop this excess would be to limit the enrollment of students in the university. This is especially difficult to do, particularly if students have the money to attend.

Unfortunately, Indian students are not like Americans, who seem to wish to stand on their own feet as soon as possible, no matter what kind of jobs they obtain. The young people of India, while similar to their parents in other respects, do not have a sense of private enterprise. The young people of India believe the government should create jobs. There is a strong dependence upon the government, and as Vinoba Bhave, the famous Gandhian philosopher and economist, once said in a public meeting, "Nowadays people utter the name 'government' more often than the name of God."

Indian students have a craze for cheap paper degrees because of the good government jobs available that require a university education. Students and parents, especially those from affluent families, believe that one has a right to obtain a university degree no matter how poor one's academic performance may be. If the colleges and universities do not yield to the demands made by students, there are strikes and sometimes riots. Parents usually support their sons in such activity, and this, in the opinion of many, is an abuse of democracy. It is a tragedy that the average Indian university student talks of a "right" when he is supposed to perform his "duty," just as he talks of duties many times when he is supposed to consider ways and means by which "rights" might be enlarged.

It should be noted that a few specialized institutions admit only first-rate students under a scholarship program. Tuition is available for these students and stipends are paid to each. One does not find these individuals showing a lack of discipline; perhaps there are two major reasons for this. One is that all the students admitted are essentially top quality and are genuinely interested in their studies. Secondly, these students are well aware of the fact that any display of poor behavior on their part might result in a cancelation of their scholarships.

In India, perhaps the solution might be to admit to university work only those students who have genuine ability to succeed, and to admit average students to types of vocational and technical training more suitable to their abilities and for that matter, to the needs of the nation.

Certainly, insofar as higher education is concerned, the ideal would be to produce as many graduates as could be employed in the respective fields of their majors. Degrees should be awarded somewhat on the basis of supply and demand.

Today the majority of university graduates hold degrees in the Humanities. It is extremely easy to take degrees in the Humanities, and it is said that most students major in this area if they cannot do well in the other colleges. In the fields of Agriculture, Medicine, and Pharmacy there is a need for more graduates. But, in the Social Sciences, or specifically in the fields of History, Languages, Literature, Politics, Anthropology, and Philosophy, there are few jobs available in India for the university graduate.

Another interesting fact about Indian higher education is the rather lengthy academic year of nine or twelve months. As a course is given over a period of nine months, with only one final examination, most of the students study seriously only for the last two or three months of each session. It has been suggested by some that the academic year be divided into three, if not four, sessions. At least the long session might be divided into two courses, with two examinations scheduled during the year. Obviously, such an innovation would approximate the semester, or the quarter system in American universities, and it would seem appropriate in view of the problems in India today.

Eventually, higher education should help transform a nation, but Indians will change the face of their nation only if they solve the problem of general lethargy. The educational system of India must be revamped in order to eliminate the lazy students and teachers. The Indian Government claims to be socialistic in principle, but it has not taken measures to force every able-bodied man to work productively.

Even with respect to university teachers, it is noted that many of them were once average or below-average students themselves. This results in maintaining both teaching and research standards at a low level. The best of the university graduates do obtain high administrative jobs within the government. These jobs afford higher salaries than do teaching jobs. Indian administrative services, for example, offer not only higher basic salary but far better increments, allowances, housing, and a host of other benefits. These are not available to university teachers, and thus those who do enter the teaching profession recognize that they are at a lower socio-economic echelon.

Even under these existing conditions, one will find a few first-rate teachers in every Indian university. Generally, these teachers are not interested in research work, but they are genuinely interested in teaching Indian youth and, in so doing, are making an intrinsic contribution to the welfare of the nation.

There has been an attempt in the foregoing to indicate how ineffective present-day higher education is in India. This paper has not meant to be overly critical, but does represent the thinking of an Indian who is concerned with analyzing the problems of education in his country, calling attention to the apparent defects, and asking for ways and means by which improvement might be effected.

The present system of education in India is as unsuited to the needs of the nation as buttons and buttonholes are to a sari. Some Indians vehemently oppose any foreign influence on the educational system. To them, we would pose a question: Has anything been learned from the historical past? What good concepts from ancient educational systems have been incorporated in the present one?

One might consider some of the good features of the ancient Nalanda University, which was established sometime in the fifth century A.D., near the present city of Patna in the Bihar State of India. Nalanda was a well-known Buddhist center. The university was run by Buddhist monks, who lived in the monasteries of Nalanda. The financial support for the university came mainly from the Hindus and various kings, who set fine examples of religious tolerance. The buildings on the campus seem to have been constructed with a definite plan, and the campus itself was about one mile in length and a half-mile in width. The buildings were magnificent. Some of them were several stories in height and indicated fine architectural design. The university acquired so much fame that many of its students came from foreign countries. Literally, it was a great *university*.

The famous seventh century Chinese traveler, Hsuan Tsang, said: "In the establishment were some thousand brethren, all men of great learning and ability, several hundreds being highly esteemed and famous; the brethren were very strict in observing the precepts and regulations of their order; learning and discussing they found the day too short, day and night they admonished each other, juniors and seniors mutually helping to perfection. Hence, foreign students came to the establishment to put an end to their doubts and then became celebrated and those who stole the name of Nalanda were all treated with respect wherever they went."

This university maintained two hundred villages as endowments. The villages were very rich. Needy students received free board and lodging, and even clothing. Sometimes for this the students had to agree to do physical work and to maintain the campus, but there were no tuition fees. The number of students exceeded five thousand by the middle of the seventh century. It is conjectured that there were roughly one thousand teachers at this time, so we can note that the ratio of teachers to students was 1 to 5, or 1 to 10 during the latter years of its operation. It seems as if most of the teachers were highly competent, and as I-tsing, another Chinese student said, "I have been very glad that I have had an opportunity of acquiring knowledge personally from them, which I should otherwise never have possessed." Only those students (regardless of their religious faith) who could pass some oral examinations were admitted, and we are told that not more than two or three of every ten taking the examinations could pass them. The main subjects taught were philosophy, law, theology, astronomy, linguistics, and medicine. The education was secular even though administration of the university was in the hands of Buddhist abbots. Under philosophy and theology, non-Buddhist schools were also taught with equal respect.

The "head" or president of the university was an abbott who was assisted by two councils. One council was responsible for admissions, courses, research work, and libraries. The second council was responsible for general administration, finance, buildings, assignment of monasteries, dormitories, arrangements for boarding, lodging, and the medical dispensary. The two councils resembled the academic and administrative councils of our modern-day universities.

The administration of the university was free from government control, even though government help was one of its main sources of income. Library facilities were wonderful; it is said that the library occupied three large buildings. Languages used were Sanskrit and Pali. But Nalanda University was destroyed about the end of the twelfth century by Muslim invaders.

I hope this paper has given you some idea of how much we can learn from our past and from your present institutions of higher learning. I have indomitable faith in the peculiar genius of the Indians that endows them with the ability to carry on the varied traditions of the past while adhering to those of the present, and trying to eliminate the evils of both in order to pave the way for a bright, harmonious future. Perhaps a bit desperately, and yet with a great deal of optimism I am still able to say in the words of that great poet, Shelley:

"If winter comes, can spring be far behind?"

Russian Education: Fact and Folklore

A. M. Gustafson

Nearly spanning the vast continent of Eurasia, the Union of Soviet Socialist Republics consists of the largest land mass in the world to be designated as a single country. Its more than 8,500,000 square miles extend from the Baltic Sea on the west to the Bering Strait on the east, within sight of Alaska. It must be remembered, however, that more than half of the Soviet Union lies north of sixty degrees, north latitude, and is too far east to derive much benefit from the gulf stream which has tempered the climate of the Scandinavian countries. Moscow is on the same latitude as the middle of Hudson Bay, and the Black Sea port of Odessa is no farther south than northern Minnesota. Agriculture has suffered from both a cold climate and a scarcity of rainfall over most of its area.

Within these borders live over 220 million people divided into 177 minority groups, speaking not less than 125 languages and dialects, and worshipping in approximately forty different religions.[1] Based on the national pride of the larger ethnic groups, the Soviet Union has organized its large territory and population into fifteen political entities known as Soviet Socialist Republics, nine autonomous regions or oblasts, and ten national districts or

---

[1] U. S. Department of Health, Education and Welfare, *Education in the USSR*, Bulletin 1957, No. 14, 7. Washington: U.S. Government Printing Office, 1957.

okrugs.[2] While recognizing the cultural and linguistic heritages of these groups, through the Communist Party and its political structure the Soviet Union has repressed political, nationalistic, and religious aspirations of any ethnic group coming into conflict with the goals of the Communist Party.

The Slavs form the largest single ethnic group and comprise 75 percent of the entire population of the Soviet Union. Of this group, the largest number are the Great Russians living in the Russian Federated Socialist Republic which occupies three-fourths of the entire country. Other Slavic groups include the Ukranians, the Belorussians, and the Poles. Among the other ethnic groups are the Armenians, the Georgians, the Kirghiz, the Kazakhs, the Uzbecks, the Buryat-Mongolians, the Finns, and the Manchurians. Unlike the United States, which also has a history of many national groups and where the melting pot has (for the most part) fused them together into one people, the problem of strong national groups remains in the Soviet Union.

Education as a Product of the Revolution

Education in Tsarist Russia was designed for the few. Even elementary education was denied to the peasantry. According to M. Deineko, author of the Soviet book, *Public Education in the USSR*,

> Almost 70% of the men and about 90% of the women were illiterate. Four-fifths of all children and adolescents did not attend school. The school system was built on class principle. . . .The schools were taught in Russian; the native languages in the outlying national districts were very much neglected. Women's educational standards were very low.[3]

To show the contrast under the Soviet system, Deineko added that,

> In 1960 the USSR numbered four times as many students as Britain, F.R.G., France and Italy taken together, although the total population of these countries almost equals that of the Soviet Union. Today over 64 million Soviet people are engaged in some form of study, i.e., every third Soviet citizen studies (excluding children of pre-school age).

---

[2] *Ibid.*

[3] Deineko, *Public Education in the USSR*, 5, 6. Moscow: Progress Publishers, approximately 1963.

He stated also that "forty-eight nationalities who formerly had no written language have now developed their own written languages."[4]

Although there can be no doubt that the aims of education in the Soviet Union have been to build a communist state and society and to unify all peoples under Soviet rule, there have been differences of opinion with regard to what methods and what types of education could best accomplish these aims. Prior to the Great October Revolution of 1917, "Marxists considered education as a weapon of the bourgeoisie through which they educated themselves and their own children in order to insure their own continuing rule and domination of the masses."[5]

Friederich Engels is quoted by the Large Soviet Encyclopedia as saying, "In capitalist society, the bourgeoisie gives the workers only as much education as is in its own interest. And that indeed is not much.[6]

A fundamental objective of the communists prior to 1917 was to wrest the weapon of education away from the capitalists.

> They promised themselves that when they came into power they would make education–including university training–open to all and that they would replace other ideologies and religion by communism.[7]

Four periods of education may be identified in the history of the Soviet Union by the following types of school systems:

1. The Nine-Year Unified Labor School, 1920-1931, which emphasized the Complex System in an attempt to integrate subject matter content with labor practices without compartmentalizing knowledge into the old traditional courses that had little or no relation one to the other.
2. The seven-year and ten-year schools which were established as the result of the school reform that had its beginnings in the decree of the Party Committee of September 5, 1931.
3. The eight-year and eleven-year schools established through the enactment of the school reform law of December 24, 1958, entitled "Law on

---

[4] *Ibid.*, p. 7.
[5] U.S. Department of Health, Education, and Welfare, *Education in the USSR, op. cit.*, p. 11.
[6] Ibid., p. 12. The original citation is : Gosudarstvennyi Institut, "Sovetskaya Entisklopediya," "Pedagogika," "Bol'shaya Sovetskaya Entsiklopediya," Vol. 44, 428. Moskva: Ogiz, 1st. ed., 1939.
[7] U.S. Department of Health, Education and Welfare, *Education in the USSR*, op. cit., p. 12.

Strengthening the Ties of School with Life and on the Further Development of the System of Public Education in the U.S.S.R."

4. The eight-year and ten-year schools established by the Central Committee of the Communist Party of the Soviet Union and the Council of Ministers of the U.S.S.R. in August, 1964, to replace the eleven-year school which had failed to meet the expectations of its proponents.

The Nine-Year Labor School

Because the gymnasia, pre-gymnasia, real schools, commercial schools, and elementary schools of Tsarist Russia (although considered good for their time by western standards) were representative of authoritarian rule and of the privileged few, they were soon swept away. In their place was established the nine-year unified labor school divided into two stages: the first consisted of five years for pupils eight to thirteen years of age, and the second, of four years for those thirteen to seventeen.

Although education was to be both coeducational and compulsory for all school-age children, the lack of facilities made compulsory education impossible.[8] Preferences were given to the children of workers. The sudden increase in the number of children who were now supposedly required to attend school brought about an unrealistic situation from the standpoint of available classrooms and teachers.

During the early years of Soviet rule, there was considerable disagreement on the nature of the educational program. Lenin declared that,

> The task of the new educator is to unite teaching activities with a socialist organization of society. . . .Teachers must consider themselves as agents of communism as well as general education.

By no means did this meet with general approval by teachers, many of whom still held traditional and religious views. There were those who "held that schools should be neither bourgeois nor proletarian; they should impart knowledge useful for all pupils regardless of their origin."[9] But V. N. Shlgin, Director of the Marx-Engels Institute of Pedagogy, stated that the new labor school was

---

[8]*Ibid.*, p. 50.

[9]U.S. Department of Health, Education, and Welfare, *Education in the USSR, op. cit.*, p. 50.

> . . . not preparation for life, but life itself. . . a life common to school children and school workers, and since in life there are neither subjects nor desks, so there should be none in school; and since productive labor is the basis for life, so it must be the basis for the school commune.[10]

The prevalent opinion of certain members of the Komsomol, the youth organization representing the working classes, was that "scholarship and intellectual knowledge in general were a reflection of capitalist culture, class distinction, and bourgeois presumptuousness." Lenin, however, in a speech delivered to them on October 2, 1920, suppressed this idea by emphasizing the need for Soviet youth to learn and to surpass the bourgeoisie in culture, organizational ability, and technique and thus, in his exact words, "beat the enemy with their own stick."[11]

It was the influence of Lenin's wife, Krupskaya, and that of the Commissar of Education, Lunarcharskii, that carried the day in favor of Lenin. Even so, the fear prevailed among some teachers that to admit "all kinds of students into the school system would lower the standards, while others continued to regard general education as a capitalistic survival."[12]

Effective implementation of the educational program during the early years of the new order proved difficult. Civil war, famines, purges, and an almost complete economic collapse made educational progress nearly impossible. Schools found it necessary to close their doors, and remained closed until 1924. The advent of the New Economic Policy in 1921 gradually had a stabilizing effect upon the schools, and improvements in enrollments were noted. The census of 1926 showed that 9.3 million out of 11 million children were in school. During the period from 1920 to 1931, the ideas of John Dewey and the American experimental programs found favor and an attempt was made to adapt them to the apparent needs of the Soviet schools.[13] Well known were the Complex Programs that were to replace the old traditional textbooks. These programs were known by various names such as the Complex, the Complex Theme, the Complexes, the Complex

---

[10]*Ibid.* The original citation is: V. N. Shulgin, "Detskaya Kommuna," *Narodnoe Prosveshchenie,* 1918, Nos. 23-25.
[11]*Ibid.*
[12]*Ibid.*, p. 51.
[13]*Ibid.*

Method, the Complex System of Instruction, and Complexity. It was during the progressive period of education from 1920 to 1931 that Nadezhda Konstantnova Krupskaya was one of the leading advocates of this system and used all the terms mentioned above in her writings. She defined the concept as follows:

All material is organized around one definite core–the labor activities of man. But this core is not selected arbitrarily. Since they are established from the historical materialism point of view, it is impossible to take any other core, because the labor activities of man determine society's structure, its politics, and culture. On the other hand, we get to know and modify the laws of nature in the labor process through an approach to natural phenomena.[14]

The Complex principle was the heart and soul of the Unified Labor School.

A labor school was conceived as an organic part of a workers' republic. Studies could not be divorced from life. Three complexes, Nature, Labor, and Society were selected by the State Academic Council as the three aspects of work activities. . . .Krupskaya deplored the traditional subject-centered curriculum in the secondary schools as fragmentary. She [Krupskaya] wrote that "some children cannot make sense out of the proliferation of subjects. They do not see the meaning of the subject matter in relation to the whole pattern of life."[15]

In the Complex programs as reported by the United States Office of Education,

Children were taught that labor is the basis of human life, that collective labor is more productive and progressive than individual labor, and that nature and natural resources are not subjects of abstract study, but exist for man to harness and put to use for the common good. They were taught that the workers in capitalist countries were exploited and that only under the socialist system could workers and peasants join forces and work for mutual benefit.[16]

It was further reported that,

The Dalton Plan, evolved by Helen Parkhurst in Dalton, Massachusetts, and the project method were widely introduced. As developed in the Soviet Union, these methods required the teachers to organize the work of pupils

---

[14]John T. Zepper, "N. K. Krupskaya on Complex Themes in Soviet Education," *Comparative Education Review*, Vol. 9, No. 1, 33.

[15]*Ibid.*, p. 35.

[16]U.S. Department of Health, Education, and Welfare, *Education in the USSR, op. cit.*, p. 51.

around projects whose execution was frequently left to the child's initiative. The children worked in groups known as brigades. Testing became "collective" with each brigade leader answering for his group.[17]

The system embodied in the Complex principle was doomed to failure and some of the reasons may be seen in Krupskaya's own writings. She wrote:

There are many difficulties: here and there you see a teacher having 100-150 pupils, having to work with three sections sometimes, and still no genuine books or grants. . . . You cannot teach letter writing and reading without books and grants. All teachers are interested in how to coordinate skills with curricula. They talk about the need to create children's books and give books to teachers.[18]

Added to the difficulties noted by Krupskaya were poorly trained teachers, poor physical facilities for labor activities, misuse of methods, and the urging of some to return to bourgeois educational practices. Voices of discontent were heard. The stage was set for the second great educational reform of the communist era.

The Seven-Year and Ten-Year School

The second educational reform began with the decree of the Party Central Committee of September 5, 1931. After commending the Soviet schools for their achievements (among which was the increase of enrollment from 7,800,000 in 1914 to 20 million in 1931), the decree proceeded to enumerate their shortcomings as follows:

School instruction is not covering a broad enough field of general educational subjects, and is not coping satisfactorily with the problem of producing for the semi-professional and higher educational institutions completely literate pupils with a good mastery of the fundamentals of knowledge, i.e., physics, chemistry, mathematics, the native language, geography, etc.[19]

The decree reintroduced regular timetables and specified the subjects to be taught. The following year (1932) another decree

---

[17] *Ibid.*, p. 52.
[18] Zepper, *op. cit.*, p. 35.
[19] U.S. Department of Health, Education, and Welfare, *Education in the USSR, op. cit.*, p. 53.

was issued which prescribed more precisely the procedures to be followed, including:

1. The laboratory-brigade method of organizing school work was to be replaced by the systematic exposition of each subject.
2. Lessons were to be arranged and planned by the teacher in accordance with a strictly defined schedule.
3. Teachers were to check the program of each pupil at the end of each quarter and to give a grade in each subject.
4. The teacher's authority was again to be respected in all phases of school activity.
5. Students who behaved in hooligan fashion, insulted the teaching staff, broke school rules, and who damaged or stole school property were to be suspended for periods of one to three years.[20]

Two years later, (1934) the seven-year and ten-year schools were introduced, although compulsory seven-year education did not go into effect until 1949. Even though certain changes were brought about by the war, the school system of the Stalin era had taken shape. During the war, schools were destroyed and attendance fell off drastically. Coeducation was abolished in 176 cities, making it possible to introduce limited military training in boys' schools. In 1954, coeducation was reestablished on the basis "that separation of the sexes was inconsistent with the principle of equality of the sexes, and was unduly expensive in requiring duplication of school organization and equipment."[21]

It was the school of the 1950s that was observed by members of the NEA-sponsored tour of the American Association of School Administrators when they visited Russia in 1959. After brief visits to schools in Copenhagan and Helsinki, they arrived in Leningrad in early October under the "watchcare" of Intourist, the one and only travel agency in the Soviet Union. Half the group flew from Helsinki in a two-motor Soviet plane, the interior of which seemed old and worn in comparison with the Finnish airplane to Helsinki. The seats were hard under the cushions, the seat belts difficult to fasten. Small hard candies, small chocolate bars, and fruit drinks were served during the hour's flight to Leningrad. The country passed over was low, much of it covered by woods, but some open

---

[20]*Ibid.*
[21]*Ibid.*, p. 54.

country could be seen, with glimpses of a number of collective farms. After customs—a brief, seemingly indifferent formality—and exchanging their dollars for rubles, the visitors were taken on an Intourist bus to the Oktobrist Hotel, a worn and dreary place with ornate walls and ceilings, undoubtedly built before the Revolution. After three nights, they were moved to another hotel called the Astoria, where they were originally scheduled to stay and which, by contrast, seemed very good.

The first school visited was Public School No. 153 in the City of Leningrad, representative of the schools in other parts of the Soviet Union. This school had been built in 1955 but seemed to be a very old building. It was a two-story structure, housing 1,200 students in grades one through ten. Seventy percent of its fifty-six teachers had come directly from the Pedagogical Institute (or teachers' college), with the result that most of the teaching staff were still in their twenties. According to the director, the fact that the young teachers had so much enthusiasm was one of the reasons the school was successful, but he said he also had some experienced teachers. Class sizes ranged from thirty-one to thirty-six in the incomplete secondary and the secondary, and as many as forty in the primary rooms. This was the school organization developed during the Stalin era and consisted of three levels: (1) primary, grades one through four; (2) incomplete secondary, grades five through seven; and (3) secondary, grades eight through ten. Compulsory attendance began at age seven and (in the old ten-year school) extended through the seventh year. Completion of eight years is now the new requirement.

The first class visited was a sixth-grade class in English. In 1959, foreign language study was not started until the fifth year, but it is now required of all students beginning in the fourth year, with offerings in English, German, and French. A choice made by the parents of a student becomes a requirement for the remainder of the time the student spends in school. English is the foreign language most often elected. This class was second-year English and the lesson consisted of reading sentences in English and translating them into Russian. Following is a simple exercise in English conversation:

Q. What is this?
A. This is a table.

Q. What is this?
A. This is a chair.
Q. What can we see on the table?
A. I see a pen and pencil on the table.

The physical characteristics of this classroom were undoubtedly indicative of all other classrooms throughout the country. In the front of the room hung the inevitable picture of Lenin. The unattractive tan walls were unevenly painted and badly in need of cleaning. To simulate a baseboard, an uneven strip of brown paint had been applied, and rows of double seats were fastened to the floor. A brown chalkboard, small in comparison to ours, was also on the front wall, and a small bulletin board near the front of the room served for the posting of notices. Eight plain light bulbs hung from the ceiling, seldom lit even on cloudy days, and plants in the windows, typical of many European school rooms, added one bright touch. The boys and girls sat together, wearing their red pioneer scarves.

The general activities of a classroom were described in the report published by the School Administrators Group after its return from Russia. Quoted from the section entitled "The Classroom" is the following:[22]

The typical Soviet classroom is teacher-dominated. Usually, the 40-to 50-minute class begins with a review of assigned homework. Sometimes this is accomplished by a question-and-answer period; sometimes, by having one or more students recite a detailed account of what has been read. Generally, the pupils involved are immediately told their grades in front of the class, and the grades are recorded in their "diaries" and in the teacher's record book. If a student falters, the teacher calls on another pupil who adds the required information while the first student remains standing. All pupils stand to recite.

Following the homework review, the teacher often spends 15 or 20 minutes in a further discussion of the topic that includes new material to be learned. In mathematics classes, pupils often do a problem while another pupil, or the teacher does the same problem at the board. Pupils doing board work are required to explain their work to the class and the teacher as they go along. It is probably significant that the pupils at their seats never question work being done at the board unless the teacher calls on one of them to correct an error. In one class, the administrators observed a pupil at the board

[22]Division of Travel Service, National Education Association, *A Firsthand Report on Soviet Schools,* 14-16. Washington, D.C.: National Education Association, 1960.

make an obvious arithmetical error (510 ÷ 2=205) and yet no one in the class raised a hand. It was noted by another visitor that three pupils near him had done the work correctly on their own papers, but let the board error go uncorrected.

Following the teacher's discussion, another question-and-answer period often ensues, with all questions being asked by the teacher. Sometimes a complete review of the teacher's statement is given by just one pupil. And in one biology class that was visited the teacher talked for about 15 minutes on the role of certain antibiotics; one pupil then came forward and reviewed the entire lecture with occasional assistance from classmates.

The announcement of the assignment for the following day generally completes the classroom cycle. Most assignments involve reading in the textbook. No supplementary books were in evidence, and no work in research books was noted by the American superintendents.

Of course, certain courses vary in method as a result of their subject matter. Classes in foreign languages involve reading and reciting from the textbook. Very little oral discussion takes place, and most of the teacher's questions are of a factual nature, such as "Who was Martin Eden?" and "What did Martin Eden want?"

Classes in the sciences often involve a teacher demonstration, in which a pupil sometimes assists. The demonstrations are set up in advance, are well planned, and are usually effective. They generally review a principle from the homework assignment or preview the next day's assignment. "Laboratory work" generally consists of a demonstration by the teacher. Pupils are called on to give details of principles. While lip service is given to "student laboratory experiments," they are not commonly carried on. In fact, many rooms are without the necessary equipment to carry out extensive pupil laboratory work. Furthermore, all pupils are assigned to do the same work. Activities at the Soviet youth organization centers, however, provide opportunities for more extensive individual and group work in zoology, botany, and similar fields.

Elementary classrooms are "self-contained": one teacher continues with the same class for the four years. Subject matter is taught in periods, and there are regular time breaks between classes.

Classes in physical culture are principally involved in exercises of various sorts. "Labor" classes actually are classes in industrial arts; all pupils in any given class work on the same project.

In a subject such as algebra, which is introduced early and studied by all pupils, the methods in use appear effective, since most pupils seem competent in this field and can substitute and solve problems freely by the time they reach grades 7 and 8.

While one professor in a pedagogical institute stated to the American superintendents that "debate is encouraged" and "differences of opinion are sought," there was no evidence of this in any of the classrooms.

In summary, it may be said that teaching methods in the classes are characterized by teacher lectures, recitations by pupils, teacher demonstrations, factual question-and-answer periods, and review of assigned work. There is no evidence of individual research on the pupil's part, of classroom discussions, or of teacher-pupil planning.

Except for a choice in foreign language when more than one is offered, there are no electives in the Soviet curriculum. The same courses are required of all students regardless of ability or aptitude. The chart on the following page shows the Soviet curriculum from grades one through ten in the ten-year school; a curriculum that was so highly praised by some critics of American schools. It is true that five years of algebra, geometry, and physics are offered beginning in the sixth grade, and four years of chemistry beginning in the seventh year, but it is difficult to equate them with courses in our own schools. Classes do not meet every day. For example, the class in algebra meets only two days a week in the sixth, seventh, and tenth years, and three times a week in the eighth and ninth years; chemistry meets twice a week in the seventh, eighth and ninth years, and four times during the tenth year; and the class in physics, which seems to receive more emphasis, meets twice a week in the sixth, three times in the seventh and eighth, and four times in the ninth and tenth years.

Not included in the curriculum chart, nor in the public schools, are the nurseries or creches, and the kindergartens. Attendance is not compulsory, but in urban areas most children attend both. Infants are placed in the nurseries from age two and one-half months to three years, and in the kindergartens from age three to seven. The nurseries are usually provided by industrial plants and are under the supervision of the Ministry of Health. The kindergartens are under the Ministry of Education and are operated by either the Ministry or by factories and collective farms.

Social Studies in the Soviet Union

Special mention is made of social studies in the Soviet Union inasmuch as they serve not only as a means to give students a knowledge and understanding of the physical, social, and political world but to indoctrinate them in the teachings of Marx and Lenin. The study of geography begins in the fourth year and lasts through the ninth. History also begins in the fourth year, but is taught in all of the remaining grades of the ten-year school.

TYPICAL SOVIET TEN-YEAR CURRICULUM

Hours per Week in Each Grade

Subject	I	II	III	IV	V	VI	VII	VIII	IX	X	Total
Russian Lang. and Lit.	13	13	13	9	9	8	6	5	4	4	2,856
Arithmetic	6	6	6	6	6	6					
Algebra						2	3	3	2	2	
Geometry						2	3	3	2	2	2,023
Trigonometry									2	2	
Physics						2	3	3	4	4	527
Chemistry							2	2	2	4	340
Astronomy										1	34
Geography				2	3	2	2	2½	3		493
History				2	2	2	2	3½	3½	4½	663
Foreign Lang.					4	4	3	3	3	3	680
Physical Ed.	2	2	2	2	2	2	2	3	3	3	782
Nat. Science or Biology				2	2	2	3	2	1		408
Psychology	(offered in only a few schools)									1	(34)
Drawing	1	1	1	1	1	1					204
Drafting							1	1	1	1	136
Singing	1	1	1	1	1	1					204
Handcrafts	1	1	2	2	2	2	2				408
Fundamentals of Production								3	4	4	374
Practical Work					x	x	x	x	x		294
Excursions	(time spread through all grades)										191
TOTALS	24	24	24	26	32	32	32	34	34	34	10,617

A number of textbooks are written in English for use in the English language schools. Two of these are *Geography of the Parts of the World and of the Most Important Countries* for the sixth grade and the first half of the seventh, by P. N. Stchastnev and

P. G. Terekhov, and *Modern History* for the ninth grade, by A. V. Efimov. The preface of the text on geography explains to students the purposes of that course as follows:

In the fifth form you received an elementary knowledge of physical geography; a general idea of the globe, of its surface and the natural phenomena occurring on it. In the sixth and the first half of the seventh form a new course of geography will be taken up—that of the parts of the world and of the most important countries in them. As you make the acquaintance of each part of the world, you will learn its specific nature. You will be given interesting facts about great travelers and explorers. You will get to know how people in other lands live and work and what large countries there are in the world. . . .

The study of different countries will lead to a better understanding of the course of events in the world today. You will learn more about the successes of socialist construction in countries of the socialist commonwealth, about the increasing struggle of the world's oppressed for freedom and independence, about the decline of the chief capitalist states and their loss of power and influence.[23]

The opening paragraph of *Modern History* reads as follows:

We are witnessing today the break-up of the capitalist system, which is the last social system based on the exploitation of man by man. To quote from the programme of the Communist Party of the Soviet Union—socialism has triumphed in the Soviet Union and has achieved decisive victories in the People's Democracies; socialism has become the practical cause of hundreds of millions of people and the banner of the revolutionary movement of the working class throughout the world.

With the building of socialism now completed, the Soviet Union has turned to the building of a communist society. In 1961 there was convened in the Kremlin the 22nd Congress of the Communist Party, rightly known as the congress of builders of communism. This congress was devoted to detailed and practical consideration of the ways of building a communist society, of planning the development of industry and agriculture, and raising the cultural level of the people.

Man has had to travel a long, long road, a road of heroic revolutionary battles, of glorious victories and temporary setbacks, a road drenched with blood of those who fought for the happiness of mankind, before he was at last able to undertake the building of a communist society.[24]

It is interesting to read other specific paragraphs in these two texts concerning the United States. In a section of the first textbook

---

[23]P. N. Stchastnev, and P. G. Terekhov, *Geography of the Parts of the World and of the Most Important Countries,* 3. Moscow: Publishing House, Prosveshcheniye, 1964.

[24]A. V. Efimov, *Modern History*, 3. Moscow: Publishing House, Prosveshcheniye, 1965.

mentioned, entitled "Brief Survey of the Countries of America," the following may be read:

The United States is the richest and most highly developed capitalist country in the world. It is at the same time the greatest exploiter of the peoples, the chief stronghold of present-day colonialism, the creator of numerous hotbeds of war in different parts of the world.[25]

A few pages later, the Soviet student reads and recites back to his teacher the content of the paragraphs below.

This wealth [industrial and agricultural], however, belongs not to the great mass of people but to the big capitalists and landowners, who have farms and ranches hundreds of hectares in size. The small farmers are constantly undergoing ruin and the number of farms is growing smaller.

There is a sharp contrast between the enormous riches of the few billionaires, who own billions of dollars, and the poverty of the rest of the people. The workers suffer from unemployment, big taxes, high prices, high rent and backbreaking toil at sweat-shops and plants.

Especially hard is the life of the Negroes, who work as labourers or metayers on the southern plantations and do the heaviest and dirtiest work at factories and plants for less pay than white workers. In many places, especially in the South, Negroes are not allowed to study at the same schools or ride in the same trams and trains as whites. They are sometimes lynched on false charges by angry crowds of racists.

The entire power of the United States rests in the hands of a small group of multimillionaires. Nowhere in the world is capitalism so powerful. The press, schools, cinemas, and television broadcastings are used to impress on the minds of the common people that Money is all-powerful. Many capitalist countries receive loans and bribes from the United States and are, therefore, completely dependent on that country.[26]

From *Modern History* the student learns,

In the meantime, harsh exploitation of the workers caused a continuous stream of them from the industrial towns in the North-East to flow toward the Indian territories of the West. There were two such streams of settlers: these were the wealthy plantation owners of the South with their slaves, and the poor migrants of the northern states who yearned for a bit of land where they could run their own farms. Here is a description of a poor family on their wesward trek: "The man hitches himself to the wagon and pulls it along, holding on to the shafts, his son giving him a helping hand, while his wife sits in the wagon and the old woman walks beside it with a gun on her shoulder, leading a cow."[27]

---

[25] Stchastnev and Terekhov, *op. cit.*, p. 239.
[26] *Ibid.*, pp. 246-248.
[27] Efimov, *op. cit.*, pp. 218-219.

A paragraph on Lincoln reads as follows:

Abraham Lincoln (1809-1865) was born in Kentucky into the family of a poor and illiterate pioneer farmer. Their neighbor, a wealthy plantation owner and slave-holder, took a dislike to the Lincoln family because of their friendly attitude towards Negroes, and began to make life hard for them, finally forcing Lincoln's father to sell his farm and move into the newly opened territories of the West. . . .[28]

The Eight-Year and Eleven-Year Schools

On December 24, 1958, the Supreme Soviet enacted a new fundamental law on education entitled "Law on Strengthening the Ties with Life and on the Further Development of the System of Education in the U.S.S.R." The Soviet Government had emphasized the need for ever greater numbers of young people trained not only in general educational subjects, but in the techniques and vocations of a changing industrial society. As early as October, 1952, high officials in the Nineteenth Congress of the Communist Party of the Soviet Union had called for more practical training of youth along polytechnical lines. Recommendations again were made in 1956 by the Twentieth Party Congress and in 1958 Nikita Khrushchev lent his strong support to the recommended reforms. In an address to the Komsomol Congress in April of that year, he said that young people ought "to know how to hold a hammer and not to confuse the handle with the claws." In a statement to the Presidium of CPSU Central Committee in September, 1958, he said: "A portion of those who finish the ten-year school unwillingly go to work in factories, plants, and collective and state farms, and some even consider that it is an insult to them." Too many students were being trained in the academic and pre-university line, and not enough in the vocational and industrial areas of education. The casual observer in the Soviet Union would tend to agree with this last statement as he views the poorly constructed building and the shoddy wares on sale in the stores.

Perhaps the solution seemed too easy. The plan that was tried experimentally in fifty schools in 1958 was a work-study program in which students spent approximately one-third of their time on the farm or in the factory, depending on whether they lived in a

[28] *Ibid.*, pp. 223-224.

rural or an urban area. One year was added to the curriculum to extend the total number of years to eleven. Compulsory education was now the completion of the eighth year. The words "we must bring the schools closer to life" and "theory closer to practice" were heard over and over again. The transition was to be completed by 1963, but in November, 1962, when a group sponsored by the Comparative Education Society, the National School Boards Association, and the International Commission of Phi Delta Kappa visited Kiev, questions were asked concerning the success and progress of the new plan. The answers seemed to indicate a continued enthusiasm for the new eleven-year school since 50 percent of the schools were then on the new plan, and by the following year, the transition was to be complete. However, not later than 1963 reports began to appear that were critical of the results of the new plan. In the April 24, 1963, issue of *Komsomolskaya Pravda*, one student wrote: "The whole of last year they taught us how to take engines apart, but we did not learn how to put them together again."[29] In the January 18, 1964, issue of the same paper, a collective letter by school directors in Moscow asked the following questions:

> Is it sensible to spend three years teaching trades which the more or less educated youths can assimilate in a matter of three or four months? Should pupils be provided with a specialty in which they have no intention of working?[30]

In November, 1965, Dr. William H. E. Johnson, director of the 1959 tour of the School Administrators, was in Moscow on leave from his position as professor of comparative education at the University of Pittsburgh. When he was asked the real reasons why the Soviets had gone back to the ten-year school, he listed these four:

1. The teachers did not like it as they felt that educational standards had been lowered. It was difficult for them to build their school schedule around the factory schedule.
2. The parents did not like it for they could not understand why their children needed experience in the factory or on the farm because they had other plans for them.

---

[29] Jaan Pennar, "Five Years After Krushchev's School Reform," *Comparative Education Review*, Vol. 8, No. 1, 75.

[30] *Ibid.*

3. The factories did not like it because it caused their production to go down in the attempt to have students do part of the work. They were in the way.
4. The students did not like it because they did not see why they should have to take the time off to do something in which they were not interested.

The New Ten-Year School

The eleven-year school had been tried and found wanting. A fourth major educational reform in less than fifty years was put into effect. In August, 1964, the ten-year school was reestablished. Some of the advantages anticipated in the eleven-year school were retained–polytechnical training was increased within the school itself; factories agreed to put equipment in the schools and improved the quality of training available. In this, a distinct improvement was noted over the old ten-year school. Many new schools had been constructed since 1959, and furnishings and equipment in general seemed better. Some of the enthusiasm of 1959 may have been lost, perhaps because the Soviets were then launching forth on a brave new venture in which all problems were to be solved by bringing schools closer to life and theory closer to practice, or so it seemed in many meetings with directors and teachers. This plan had failed, and it may be that educators now view the role of the schools more realistically than before.

Criticism of Soviet Education in the U.S.S.R.

At no time during the half century of communist rule have the Soviets been completely satisfied with their schools. We have noted the dissatisfaction with the early progressive system which employed the Complex methods. The ten-year school established during the Stalin era was modified during Khrushchev's leadership in an attempt to bring schools closer to the realities of life by providing for more practical education for youth. It was the old ten-year school that was praised so highly by Admiral Rickover, Arthur Bestor, and by others.

What did the Soviets themselves have to say about their schools at the time that some of our countrymen were regarding Soviet education as superior to ours? In the research by Richard Lee Renfield, published in 1959 by the Educational Policies Commission of the National Education Association when he was project secretary, Renfield wrote the following under the title "Soviet Doubts About the Quality of Learning":

It is true that Ten-Year School graduates have taken more years of science, mathematics, and foreign language than the average American high school graduate. But Soviet educators often demonstate a painful awareness that a course taken cannot necessarily be equated with knowledge acquired. For one thing, much is forgotten immediately after graduation.[31]

For another, much is not learned in the first place.[32]

The director of the Laboratory on Methods of Physics Instruction of the Institute for Teaching Methods of the Academy of Pedagogical Sciences of the RSFSR reports:

Tests given in the ninth and tenth grade classes in Moscow and in Penza, Kemerovo, and Novosibirsk Regions provided a glaring example of the inadequacy of the knowledge of physics possessed by secondary-school graduates. The tests indicated that upper-graders have little understanding of such important and widely applied concepts as work, energy, power, efficiency, and commit gross errors in the measurements of physical quantities.[33]

An inspector of the Central School Administration of the Ministry of Education of the RSFSR writes:

During school inspections in two cities, Orenburg and Lower Troitsk, and four districts, Sorochinsk, Totsk, Saraktash, and Chkalov, in order to obtain objective data on pupil achievement, the inspectors administered arithmetic tests to grades four and five, algebra and geometry tests to grades seven and eight, and geometry tests to grade ten. The tests were of average, and in some cases below average, difficulty. [The emphasis of the tests was different for various classes of the same grade] .

In most cases, the marks which had been given by the teachers were at sharp variance with those received on the inspectors' tests. . . . For example, one teacher at Secondary School No. 8 in Lower Troitsk was giving passing marks to all his eighth-grade pupils, but 70% of his pupils failed the inspectors' test. . . . Grading by some teachers. . . is characterized by liberalism.[34]

---

[31]Richard Lee Renfield, *Soviet Criticism of Soviet Education Some Aspects of the Ten-Year School Which Certain Americans Have Praised,* pp. 45-46. Washington: The National Education Association, 1959.

[32]N. K. Goncharov, "The Building of Communism and the School," *Soviet Pedagogy*, XXII, Dec. 1958, 50.

[33]V. Yus'kovich, "Improving Physics Teaching in the Secondary School," *Public Education*, Sept. 1958, 50.

[34]I. Kudinov, "Serious Defects in Mathematics Teaching," *Public Education*, Oct. 1958, 45-46.

Renfield found in Soviet education journals that there were many other indications of low-level learning in the ten-year school. For example:

1. According to an order of the Ministry of Education of the RSFSR, "The general level of mathematical preparation of pupils in the general-education schools falls short of modern requirements, and mathematics teaching in many schools is unsatisfactory.[35]
2. In a review of literature published by pedagogical institutes, the reviewer observes that lack of attention in arithmetic and mathematics courses to the development of mathematical thought has resulted in the following situation: "Though they know by heart many theorems, formulas, and rules of geometry, alegebra, and arithmetic, pupils are unable to apply them to proofs, examples, or particularly problems."[36]
3. According to a methods specialist in the Central School Administration of the Ministry of Education of the RSFSR, the geography course too frequently consists of "mechanical memorization of textbooks and maps, as a result of which pupils' knowledge is an accumulation of disconnected facts."[37]
4. An inspector of the Central School Administration of the Ministry of Education of the RSFSR tells of "the inability of many students to generalize about or to see cause-effect relationships among historical phenomena."[38]
5. A methods specialist in the Central School Administration of the Ministry of Education of the RSFSR complains that many tenth-graders display little understanding of literature they study, although "they give confident textbook answers in class."[39]

It seems evident that Soviet school leaders did not have as high regard for their own educational system as did certain critics of American education. The Soviets are still dissatisfied with their school program. As recently as November, 1966, the Central Committee of the Communist Party ordered a major curriculum revision to be ready by 1970. *Time* (December 30, 1966),

---

[35]Ministry of Education in RSFSR, "On the State of and Means of Improving the Teaching of Mathematics in the Schools of the RSFSR," April, 1957, quoted by I. Kudinov, "Serious Defects in Mathematics Teaching," *Public Education*, Oct. 1958, 44.

[36]P. V. Titkov, "The Scholarly Notes of Pedagogical Institutes," *Soviet Pedagogy*, XXII, 144, Dec. 1958.

[37]V. Tutochkina, "Teaching Georgraphy," *Public Education*, Sept. 1958, 56.

[38]A. Tyutin, "In History Class," *Public Education*, Feb. 1958, pp. 69-70.

[39]M. Shil'nikova, "Raising the Level of Literature Instruction," *Public Education*, Sept. 1958, p. 53.

reported an article in *Pravda* earlier in December written by the Russian Minister of Education, Mikhail Prokofiev, explaining the action of the Central Committee. Prokofiev "charged that the vast Soviet school system is not only seriously deficient in 'science and math teaching', but is mired in a rigid 'bookism' that makes learning a bore and produces an alarming dropout rate." According to *Time*, he complained that "students spend from 24 to 30 hours a week taking lecture notes, which allows them 'far too little time' to develop their own initiative, to stimulate creative work." He is also concerned with the serious teacher shortage which the Soviet Union apparently faces. He admitted that, with the lowering of standards for entrance to teacher-training academies, more than half of the 116,000 students who entered last fall "barely passed the entrance examinations." Such teachers cannot and do not keep pace with technological advances. In physics for example, they give their students "what amounts to history of the subject" instead of bringing them face to face with the core of physics itself. *Time* reports,

> The net result is that many students are convinced "that they are not receiving any profound and lasting education. They want to quit." The dropout rate has reached the point where 30% of the pupils who enter first grade do not finish eighth. In some regions, half of those who finish eighth grade fail to enter the two-year high schools. And of those who finish high school, only 20% are interested enough to go on to universities and professional institutes.[40]

The self-criticism by the Soviets seems to indicate that they are aware of the shortcomings in their educational system and that they intend to do something about them.

Moving Forward

The Soviets have done a number of things that indicate progress. In 1958 it was reported there were seventeen experimental language schools in the larger cities of the Soviet Union for the purpose of producing students fluent in foreign languages; eight of these were in English, seven in German, and two in

---

[40] *Time* (Dec. 30, 1966) 33.

French.[41] By 1965, forty special language schools in English had been established in Moscow alone. Eighteen other special schools had been set up for other foreign languages and mathematics and science.

Admission of pupils to special language schools is very selective and is based on an oral admission test in Russian designed to uncover those with a proficiency in language. In one special English ten-year school, only seventy-two of approximately four hundred applicants are enrolled each year. This results in a superior student body. English is taught as a second language, beginning in the second year. Social studies are taught beginning with the fifth year and science and mathematics beginning with the eighth year. It was observed that students in the English language school had a better knowledge of English than did those in the regular day schools.

The improvement noted in the polytechnical classes of the new ten-year school is believed to be significant. Materials and equipment had improved. As noted earlier, the factories had put equipment into the schools after the decision was made to give up the eleven-year plan. The lumber used in woodshop classes, however, would not come up to standards in this country. The need for students to take vocational courses is recognized as much now as it was at the time of the School Reform Act of 1958. The attempt to bring the schools closer to life is now being made in the schools rather than in the factories and on the farms. One school visited in Moscow was well supplied with equipment for teaching business machine procedures and one classroom was devoted to teaching of data processing; it served also as a data processing center.

Youth activities, although separate from the schools, merit comment because of their excellence, and because, to a large extent, they support the educational programs of the schools. Pioneer palaces and pioneer houses or homes serve the three communist youth organizations: the Octobrists, age 7 to 10; the Pioneers, age 10 to 15; and the Komsomol (Young Communist

---

[41] U.S. Department of Health, Education, and Welfare, *Soviet Commitment to Education*, 35. Washington: U.S. Government Printing Office, 1959.

League), age 15 to 26. In the large new Pioneer Palace in Moscow, a short distance from the University, it was noted that sixteen thousand young people participated in eight hundred groups in activities that included nearly every interest or activity of benefit to boys and girls and young adults. Circle or club activities included such interests as mathematics, science, astronomy, radio, music, dancing, drama, literature, chess, stamp collecting, and model airplanes. Here the talented and gifted found opportunities not provided by the schools. In the Pioneer Palace alone were eight hundred full-time workers, some of whom worked in the summer camp programs. In addition, in other parts of Moscow seventeen pioneer houses provided for smaller numbers of youth. Similar programs were carried on in all the large population centers of the U.S.S.R.

There can be no doubt that the Soviets intend to move forward in the field of education. And we must be impressed by the confidence, the sense of direction, and the dedication of many of the Soviet educators. At the same time, however, we are imbued with an even greater appreciation of the accomplishments of our own school system.

Biobliography

A Firsthand Report on Soviet Schools. Washington, D.C.: National Education Association, Division of Travel Service (1960), pp. 14-16.

Deineko, M. *Public Education in the USSR.* Moscow: Progress Publishers (approximately 1963).

Efimov, A. V. *Modern History*. Moscow: Publishing House, Prosveshcheniye, 1965.

Goncharov, N. K. "The Building of Communism and the School," *Soviet Pedagogy*, XXII (December 1958).

Kudinov, I. "Serious Defects in Mathematics Teaching," *Public Education* (October 1958).

"On the State of and Means of Improving the Teaching of Mathematics in the Schools of the RSFSR." Ministry of Education in RSFSR (April 1957). Quoted by I. Kudinov, "Serious Defects in Mathematics Teaching," *Public Education* (October 1958).

Pennar, Jaan. "Five Years After Khrushchev's School Reform," *Comparative Education Review,* VIII, No. 1, 75.

Renfield, Richard Lee. *Soviet Criticism of Soviet Education, Some Aspects of the Ten-Year School Which Certain Americans Have Praised*, pp. 45-48. Washington, D.C.: National Education Association (1959).

Shil'nikova, M. "Raising the Level of Literature Instruction," *Public Education,* September 1958.

Stchastnev, P.N. and Terekhov, P. H. *Geography of the Parts of the World and of the Most Important Countries.* Moscow: Publishing House, Prosveshcheniye, 1964.

Time, December 30, 1966, p. 33.

Titkov, P.V. "The Scholarly Notes of Pedagogical Institutes," *Soviet Pedagogy,* XXII, December 1958.

Tutochkina, V. "Teaching Geography," *Public Education,* September 1958.

Tyutin, A. "In History Class," *Public Education,* February 1958.

U. S. Department of Health, Education, and Welfare. *Education in the USSR.* Washington, D.C.: U.S. Government Printing Office, 1957.

U.S. Department of Health, Education, and Welfare. *Soviet Commitment to Education*. Washington, D.C.: U.S. Government Printing Office, 1959.

Yus'kovich, V. "Improving Physics Teaching in the Secondary School," *Public Education*, September 1958.

Zepper, John T. "N.K. Krupskaya on Complex Themes in Soviet Education," *Comparative Education Review,* IX, No. 1, 33.